HUNTING SHADOWS

MIRROR BOOKS

© Jane Hamilton

The rights of Jane Hamilton to be identified as the author of this book have been asserted, in accordance with the Copyright, Designs and Patents Act 1988.

All rights reserved. No part of this publication may be reproduced, stored in a retrieval system, or transmitted, in any form or by any means without the prior written permission of the publisher, nor be otherwise circulated in any form of binding or cover other than that in which it is published and without a similar condition being imposed on the subsequent purchaser.

1

Published in Great Britain and Ireland in 2026 by Mirror Books, a Reach PLC business.

www.mirrorbooks.co.uk
@TheMirrorBooks

Print ISBN 9781917439718
eBook ISBN 9781917439725

Cover Design: Chris Collins
Editing and Production: Christine Costello

Every effort has been made to trace copyright. Any oversight will be rectified in future editions.

Printed and bound in Great Britain by
CPI Group (UK) Ltd, Croydon, CR0 4YY

HUNTING SHADOWS
JANE HAMILTON

MIRROR BOOKS

For Vicky, Dinah & Angelika, and for all the women who never got to tell their own stories.

CONTENTS

Foreword	7
Author's Note	11
The Call	14
Vicky	17
Dinah	35
Angelika	45
A Drifter Called Pat	62
The Man Who Learned To Vanish	68
The Body In The Church	77
The Man Behind The Name	87
First Wives – First Warnings	93
Cathy	113
Daniel	125
The Angelika Kluk Trial: Part One	140
The Angelika Kluk Trial: Part Two	155
The Damage Done	165
The Missed Chance	173
The Birth Of Operation Anagram	182
Back In The Dock	188
The Final Trial	198
Unfolding The Anagram	209
Sorting Fact From Folklore	224
The Ghost Of Bible John	236

The Hunt	249
Wider Shadows – The World's End	266
Could There Be Another Tobin?	282
Cuts, Cuts, Cuts	294
The Weight Of Witness	303
Epilogue	315
Acknowledgements	317

FOREWORD

BY THE MOST cursed of coincidences, Central Scotland was stalked by no less than three serial killers in the decades leading up to the millennium.

The concentration of such serious offenders led many to believe they must be connected.

Even the FBI, the originators of the title serial killer, believed that it was "statistically improbable" that such singular offences, in such a tight timescale and geographical location, were unconnected. There was no connection between Angus Sinclair, Robert Black, and Peter Tobin. Lengthy investigation found no evidence that they ever met, let alone collaborated in crime.

Sinclair, the World's End Killer, was the most prolific of the three, offending between 1977 and 1980, if you ignore a childhood conviction. Yet in that brief time he murdered three young women, certainly killed three more, and raped and assaulted a dozen children.

A highly organised predator, his crimes all fitted a tight pattern of weekend abductions, strangulation by items of the victims' clothing, the depositing of his victims' bodies at quiet rural locations known to Sinclair.

Only groundbreaking forensic science eventually tracked him down in 2004, and it took changes to the law to eventually convict him in 2014.

Black was a child snatcher, a delivery van driver who travelled and habitually offended along the trunk roads between England and Scotland, but also travelled as far as Northern Ireland and Europe. He offended between 1978 and 1996, when he was caught in the act of abducting a young girl in the Scottish Borders. A deadly hunter of children, he was eventually convicted of four child murders but was undoubtedly responsible for others. Lacking any forensic evidence, Black was convicted by a complex combination of circumstantial evidence, the result of the first structured multi force enquiry and the first use of computers in the investigation of murder.

Tobin, the subject of this book, and the last of this dreadful trio to be detected, offended between 1990 and 2006, and in many ways was the most difficult to catch. His modus operandi of keeping and concealing the bodies of his victims not only deprived investigators of the forensic opportunities that a murder victim's body can give, but also ensured that the disappearance of his first two victims, Vicky Hamilton and Dinah McNicol, remained classified as missing persons rather than murders. It may seem a fine point, but the truth is that missing persons are rarely allocated the same resources as murders.

Tobin's habit of adopting false names and moving throughout the UK also made him incredibly difficult to detect before the days of computer assisted policing, or adequate systems of communication between police forces.

Tobin's last crime, the murder of Angelika Kluk, was an uncharacteristically botched affair, lacking any of his previous

FOREWORD

planning or control of the body. In what appeared to be a chaotic attack, he lacked the means to conceal the body of his victim properly and, to make matters worse, fled the scene, instantly arousing suspicion.

Had Peter Tobin not murdered Angelika Kluk in such an amateurish way, I doubt he would ever have been caught, or the remains of Vicky and Dinah ever found.

This study into the crimes of Peter Tobin by Jane Hamilton is the fullest examination of his murderous career, and a unique insight into the author's life and work as a front line investigative journalist for over 25 years. The sensitive tasks of seeking out information, dealing with vulnerable families, and trying to balance the competing demands of hard news versus the ends of justice are all addressed with candour, empathy, and an unsparing eye for detail. This is no fairy story. It is clear that gathering the news on the front line is both emotionally and physically taxing. It is not a job for the faint hearted.

Unfortunately, this account is also something of a historical piece, for the time of experienced investigative journalism is mainly gone. The rise of social media and instant 24 hour news has led to the decline of high quality print journalism, epitomised by Jane Hamilton and her generation. The standard of our news has suffered accordingly.

In the final chapter of this excellent book, Jane asks the key question. "Given all our new technology, could predators like Peter Tobin still operate today?"

The answer must be unequivocally, yes of course. Do we really believe that Peter Tobin was unique? Or that the conditions of deprivation and violence that spawned him and the other serial killers no longer exist?

At any given time there are around 12,000 long term missing persons (missing for over a year), 5,000 of which are women. Many of these will have ducked out of sight for personal reasons, perhaps to escape some trauma. But we would be naive not to recognise that some will lie in unmarked graves, yet to be discovered, killed by predators like Tobin, yet to be identified.

Human nature dictates that killers like Tobin will always exist, and we cannot rely on technology alone to protect us.

Only constant vigilance, a practised eye, and good early warning systems will ensure that predators like Peter Tobin cannot prevail.

Tom Wood QPM is a former Deputy Chief Constable and Officer in overall command of Operation Trinity, the investigation into the Worlds End Murders and associated crimes.

AUTHOR'S NOTE

I'VE SPENT MOST of my life writing about murder. The headlines may change but the people affected don't.

Before the name Peter Tobin meant anything to anyone, there were just missing girls, grieving families and police officers who couldn't connect the dots.

I covered their stories one by one, never realising how close they were to each other or to him.

When the pattern became clear, it wasn't like a bolt of lightning. It sneaked up, as is often the way with these things. Familiar names of women whose stories I had worked on in the past, unsolved disappearances and murders, the same kind of details repeating themselves.

There was a slow, sickening recognition. The same type of victim. The same habits. The same man hiding behind different names.

For years he lived among us, he fixed fences, painted walls, mended things and helped out at churches. Ordinary enough that nobody looked twice.

But this is what predators rely on – they blend in, talk politely, hold doors open for you, smile. That fleeting thought of unease you just felt? They'll make you doubt that. Your instincts must be wrong. You brush it to one side, he's a nice man, a helpful man. And anyway, you can't quite put your finger on what's wrong. So you go about your day and 99 times out of 100 you won't hear anything bad about them. But, and there's always a but… that one time is just there.

This book isn't about glorifying Peter Tobin. It isn't about dredging up pain for the people who have already lived it. It is about learning from what happened, about how victims get forgotten, how systems fail, and how we can do better.

Every unsolved case, every missing person headline begins the same way: with a life that mattered.

Vicky Hamilton, Dinah McNicol, Angelika Kluk. Their names absolutely deserve to outlive his.

They were daughters, sisters, students, and friends. They laughed, worked, argued, and planned their futures. They were alive. That is how they should be remembered.

For me this isn't history. It is a lived memory. I was there when Angelika's body was found. I watched families hold press conferences desperate for information about daughters who never came home. I sat with their friends and family, I spoke to people close to Tobin, I spoke to detectives who couldn't let go of the case even when everyone else had moved on. These stories are stitched into the last 20 years of my working life.

Writing this book isn't about reopening wounds. It's about understanding what those wounds cost. It's about why the police built Operation Anagram to investigate Tobin's past, why journalists like me kept chasing a man most people wanted to forget, and why the victims' families still deserve better than silence. Especially the victims whose families will most likely never have the answers they need.

Scotland has its fair share of monsters, but the real story is

AUTHOR'S NOTE

how ordinary people respond to them. The detectives who don't quit. The communities that keep remembering. The families who refuse to be defined by loss.

If this book makes anything clear, I hope it's that we cannot look away. We cannot pretend these things belong to the past. Because when we do, another name appears, another story starts, and the cycle begins again.

This isn't just the story of Peter Tobin. It's a story about the people who would not let him disappear into history. The survivors, the families, the police, and the journalists who refused to stop asking questions.

Some stories stay with you because you broke them. Others stay with you because you couldn't walk away.

This one never left me.

PROLOGUE

THE CALL

PETER TOBIN WAS dead.

The news broke on a Saturday morning in October 2022. By lunchtime the story was everywhere: serial killer dies in prison, aged 76. The headlines were brief, the tone almost polite, as if death had finally tidied up what the justice system couldn't.

Driving north on the A9, heading for the Isle of Skye, my phone started ringing off the hook. Friends, journalists, old contacts, all wanting a quote or a comment. The signal cut in and out as the hills closed around me, but one call came through clearly.

Tom Fox, then the Head of Communications for the Scottish Prison Service and a good friend I still miss to this day. We had known each other since my very first day as a reporter – he was the grumpy but honest press officer with many years of experience in dealing with journalists under his belt.

I thought he was obstructive. He thought I was a brat.

But over time, we built a solid strong relationship that was based on mutual respect.

We both knew the score of the world we lived in and we knew where we stood in the worlds we worked in.

THE CALL

Tom had dealt with Tobin and enquiries about him for years. He knew what this moment meant for the families, for the detectives and for those of us who had followed the case from the start.

"You led the way on this one, Jane," his voice echoed down the line. "Maybe now the families can get some peace."

Then there was silence. Neither of us needed to say more than that.

A few weeks earlier I had taken voluntary redundancy from the *Daily Record* – 25 years of deadlines and front pages had caught up with me. I was burnt out. The last year had been difficult for personal and professional reasons and I needed a break from news and newspapers.

For the first time in decades, I wasn't chasing the next story.

So when Tobin's death broke, I didn't feel the old rush to be first with it. I didn't scramble for reaction or hunt for exclusives, I just kept driving. It felt strangely liberating that this man no longer had any power to control the narrative.

The day carried on as normal. The country didn't stop. Traffic still built up on the road north, the radio still played the news on rotation, and most people heard his name and barely remembered who he was. But for me, and for everyone who had covered those cases, it would be the end of a chapter that had lasted for far too long.

I had written about Tobin for many years. I had interviewed his wives and reported from the scenes. I spoke to the detectives who built Operation Anagram from nothing but a hunch. I had also watched the story become something else: a guessing game, a series of headlines, a true crime myth.

When I first heard his name back in 2006, I didn't know who he really was. Nobody did. He had been hiding in plain sight for decades. By the time he was convicted of murder, I had spent months knocking on doors, chasing his trail through old addresses, listening to people who still couldn't quite believe they had known him.

When he died, the official line was a simple one. He had been ill for some time and was pronounced dead at the Royal Infirmary of Edinburgh. There was no drama.

I briefly thought back to the story about him I'd broken four years before his eventual death – that he had cancer and it was unlikely he would survive it. But he endured and it seemed like even death couldn't give anyone the satisfaction of an ending.

Until it did and drew a line under one of the darkest chapters in Scottish criminal history.

I thought of the families. Of the mothers who never saw justice in their lifetimes, and the brothers and sisters who carried the weight instead. I thought of the detectives who kept going, even when it took something out of them.

And I thought of the women who survived him and still live with his shadow. Tobin's death didn't close anything. It didn't end the story. It simply meant that the man who had taken so much would never tell us how far his violence really went. He went to his grave with secrets. But secrets leave traces.

This book is about following those traces, the victims he tried to erase, the families who never stopped looking, and the investigators who refused to forget.

It begins with the people he harmed, not the man himself.

CHAPTER ONE

VICKY

THE SNOW HAD started to melt but the air was still biting. The pavements were wet and dark, the street lamps throwing long yellow shadows. Vicky Hamilton sat on a bench near Bathgate town centre with a bag of chips in her hands. Steam rose into the cold and the smell of vinegar clung to her coat.

The working-class commuter town between Edinburgh and Glasgow, like so many, had its high street lined with bookmakers, chip shops, and small, family-run stores.

The railway had reopened a few years earlier after decades of closure, linking the town again to Edinburgh. Even so, most people still relied on buses for short journeys across West Lothian. On Sunday nights the last services ran early. Most shops were shut by six, and by seven the streets thinned out apart from a few people leaving the pubs or takeaways.

The police station sat at the edge of the town centre on Hopetoun Street.

It was Sunday, 10 February 1991. Vicky was 15 and making the trip home to Redding after a weekend with her sister, Sharon, in Livingston.

It was meant to be simple, one bus to Bathgate, another on to Falkirk, then a short walk home. A small adventure, her first time doing the route back home alone.

She'd double-checked it with Sharon. She wanted things clear in her head but she was nervous.

The town had that drained feeling Sunday nights get when people know the weekend is over and it's time to start thinking about work and school. A few cars moved through the high street, tyres sloshing over wet tarmac.

A normal night, no suggestion of peril in the air and her thoughts filled with memories of the weekend with her sister.

Vicky lived in Redding with her mum, Janette and younger twin siblings, Lindsay and Lee. Her parents were separated with dad, Michael, living elsewhere, though he remained involved in the family life and would later become an important figure in keeping Vicky's story alive. Although they were a divided family, they were still close.

***

Two days earlier the snow had come down hard across West Lothian and its surrounding towns Livingston's wide roads turned white and the new town looked even fresher after the snowfall.

On Saturday, the gritters had been out, the slush gathering in grey heaps along the kerbs.

Sharon Brown had been waiting for her sister at the bus stop that Saturday morning. She saw her before she got off, the familiar flash of the schoolbag and the smile that came when Vicky spotted her. The girls hugged, stamping their feet against

VICKY

the cold. Sharon was older by a few years and was living in her own place in Livingston.

Vicky looked up to Sharon, the way younger sisters do when someone they love seems a step ahead in life.

Sharon's flat was small but bright. To Vicky it must have felt like a glimpse of what came next – independence, making her own choices one day, grown up life.

They spent the weekend the way they usually did: a wander round Livingston's Centre, the main shopping precinct built when the new town first took shape in the 70s. It was the heart of the place, a stretch of shops and cafes where everyone went on a Saturday. There was Woolworths, Boots, John Menzies, C&A – the usual mix of High Street stores popular at the time.

They tried on earrings they couldn't afford, shared chips, giggled over the magazines. They talked about school, boys, and music.

Vicky loved the idea of her future, even if she couldn't see its shape yet.

That night they watched television, flicking between programmes, swapping stories. Vicky was shy but opened up once she trusted you. She talked about school and her friends, the teachers she liked, the ones who made her nervous. Sharon noticed she kept checking her purse, counting her change for the bus home. Vicky was nervous about going home alone.

The next day, they woke late to the sound of the wind against the windows. The snow had started to thaw. Vicky sat at the table eating toast, hair pulled back, her coat already over the chair, ready to leave. Sharon brewed tea and checked the time.

"You sure you know where you're going?" she asked.

Vicky nodded and glanced at the clock again. "One to Bathgate, then Falkirk, then home." She'd said it so many times it had become a chant.

"Good girl," Sharon said. She tried to sound confident but something in her tone made Vicky laugh and reassure her sister.

"I'll be fine, honest."

Around 5pm, they walked together to the bus stop. The pavements were slick and shiny, and cars passed with slow caution.

Vicky's cheeks were pink from the cold. The bus came into view. Sharon hugged her sister tightly before she got on.

Vicky climbed aboard and waved from the window.

Sharon stood there for a moment after the bus pulled away, watching the back of it disappear around the corner.

The bus to Bathgate was mostly empty. A few older passengers sat scattered through the seats, heads bent, shopping bags between their feet. The windows fogged with condensation. Outside, the fields flashed by in shades of brown and grey, the edges of the roads lined with snow. The driver had the radio on low with static crackling between songs.

Vicky sat near the middle, her bag tucked by her feet, her fingers tapping lightly against the strap. She counted out her coins again, rehearsed the next step in her head. Bathgate, change for Falkirk, walk home from the stop. Simple. She had done it before with Sharon, but never alone.

The journey took 20 minutes. When the bus pulled into Bathgate roughly around 5.30pm, she stood, thanked the driver,

VICKY

and stepped down into the cold. The sharp air hit her face. She pulled her scarf tighter and looked around.

She walked a little way, checking the signs, then ducked into a takeaway for warmth. The man behind the counter asked what she wanted and she pointed to the chips. He poured them into the paper and shook salt over the top. She paid with the exact change, thanked him, and went back out.

As she sat on the bench with the bag cupped in her hands, the heat seeping through the paper steam curled into the air. She took a few bites, blowing on each chip to cool it.

A handful of stragglers passed her by. A couple leaving the pub, a lad with a pizza box under his arm, a woman pulling her coat tight round her shoulders. They noticed her because she was young, polite and she was asking for directions from several people.

But she was also just another teenager waiting for a bus.

Around 5.50pm, she approached a woman outside the takeaway, polite and soft-spoken, asking where to catch the Falkirk bus.

One woman said the stop was by the police station, not far, maybe a few hundred yards. Vicky thanked her and walked a little way before sitting down again. She seemed unsure.

Another woman gave directions and when it became clear the buses had stopped for the night because of the weathr, she offered to share a taxi, but Vicky declined.

Maybe she was shy. Maybe she didn't have the money to spare. Maybe she didn't want to get it wrong by taking a ride with a stranger.

She told the woman she would find her own way home.

It was the kind of decision that made perfect sense at the time.

A car slowed nearby, headlights washing over her for a moment before moving on. She looked down the street, hoping a bus would appear. None came.

The bag of chips steamed in her hands. She held it like a hot-water bottle. She watched the headlights sweep across the puddles, each one glimmering for a second before darkness closed again. She sat there for a while, the last of the daylight gone, the streetlights buzzing faintly above. A gust lifted the wrappers in the gutter and pushed the smell of fried food back towards her. The cold bit through her tights. She shifted her feet, pulled her coat tighter, and looked down the road again.

If Vicky felt uneasy, no one actually noticed. She was just a girl with a bag of chips, waiting for the bus.

Bathgate sat between two worlds. To one side was Livingston, with its new estates and a busy shopping centre with plans to turn it into a sprawling retail park. To the other, Falkirk, tired and built on the bones of old industry.

Bathgate felt somewhere between them. Rows of family-owned shops, some with their signs worn away or peeling, pubs where everyone knew each other, the same faces in the same seats. A place that was safe enough if you minded your own business.

People thought of it as ordinary because it was just an ordinary Scottish town on an ordinary, cold, Scottish winter night. It was the kind of night you forget about unless something goes wrong.

VICKY

The air tightened as the temperature dropped. Frost started to form again on the parked cars. The sound of boots on the pavement grew rarer. The last bus to Falkirk came and went.

The town had emptied. The chip shop lights went out, and the metal shutter rolled down with a rattle that echoed along the street. The only sound after that was the occasional car and the hum of the streetlights.

A few hundred yards away, a police constable on the late shift walked his usual route between the station and the high street. He noticed the cold, the stillness, how his breath hung in front of him. He didn't remember seeing Vicky.

It was only later, after 6pm, another witness saw Vicky near Bathgate Police Station.

***

In Redding, Vicky's mother was waiting for her daughter to come home.

Three miles south-east of Falkirk, it was a close-knit community of miners' rows and post-war houses. The Hamilton home sat just off the main road on Laing Crescent. Neighbours knew them well; Vicky's mother, Janette, worked locally and knew most people in the village. The family's dog, Patch, was a familiar sight in the street.

That Sunday, the quiet of the area only added to Janette's growing worry as the hours went by. The dog was curled by the fire, the radio low. Janette checked the clock and frowned. It was late, but not so late it couldn't be explained away. Maybe Vicky had missed her connection, maybe the snow was slowing the traffic. She lit a cigarette and stubbed it out half-finished. Something in her chest felt off.

The television was on. Janette checked the time again. Vicky should have been home by now. It was 7pm and the journey usually only takes just under an hour.

By 8pm the streets in Redding were empty.

Janette kept telling herself the buses were late, the weather was slowing everything down, but she couldn't settle. She moved from room to room, straightening things that didn't need it, switching the kettle on and off without realising.

Janette stood at the window waiting for Vicky. Her daughter was never careless with time. She liked to know where she was meant to be, when she was meant to be there. Janette knew that. The longer the night went on, the more Janette started to feel uneasy.

She phoned Sharon. The call connected. Sharon answered quickly.

"She's not back yet," Janette said.

"What do you mean, not back? She left hours ago."

"She's probably just missed her connection."

Sharon paused. "She'd have called."

Both women sat with the receiver pressed to their ear, saying nothing for a moment, hearing only the sound of each other breathing.

Janette forced a small laugh, trying to sound calm. "Buses, weather, you know what it's like."

Sharon didn't answer straight away. "Aye, but she'd have called," she said again, quieter this time.

VICKY

When Janette hung up, the house felt colder. The dog stirred, unsettled by her movements.

She went back to the window and lifted the net curtain slightly. The street outside was still, just a line of parked cars and a dim glow from the lamppost. Still no sign of her daughter.

By 11pm she was pacing the living room, watching for headlights. When the phone rang she jumped. It was Sharon.

"Mum, I've called the bus depot and the police. They're looking into it."

Janette told her she would phone the local station herself.

The constable who answered took the details, when Vicky had left, what she was wearing, who she was visiting. He told her it was probably nothing serious. Girls that age stayed out sometimes.

Janette said her daughter wasn't like that.

He noted the call and said a patrol car would check the route between Bathgate and Falkirk.

When she hung up, she felt sick. The house was too quiet and the clock too loud. Where was Vicky?

At midnight she called the police again and they came not long after.

Two uniformed officers stood in the doorway, notebooks in hand, asking the usual things.

"When did you last speak to your daughter, Mrs Hamilton?"

"She phoned from Livingston before she left. She was getting the bus. She should've been home hours ago."

"Any reason she might have stayed somewhere else?"

"No. She'd have called."

They noted it all, and promised to check bus stations and hospitals. Janette watched them go. Her fear had turned to something harder.

Through the night, Janette continued to phone the station for updates. Each time she was told there was no news but that patrols were still out checking. She thanked them, hung up, and stayed awake until morning.

The police returned just after eight the next morning. It was the same two officers, looking tired now. They asked if they could see a recent photograph. She passed over Vicky's school photo. Short bob, wide smile, wearing her school uniform.

None of them knew but it was to become a picture everyone would come to recognise.

The officers nodded, thanked her, and said they'd be in touch and left.

Lunchtime came and the neighbours already knew. Redding wasn't the kind of place where news travelled slowly. People rallied round, offering to search for Vicky, make sandwiches, anything that felt useful.

People meant well but bad news or gossip travels fast and quite often it takes on a life of its own. Everyone had a theory.

That evening, officers began walking the main routes between Livingston, Bathgate and Redding, checking verges and bus stops, asking drivers if they had seen her.

They checked old railway lines and the edge of the Union canal. They knocked on doors, they stopped cars and asked drivers if they'd seen a girl on her own, brown hair, carrying a school bag. No one had.

VICKY

Sharon came home to Redding the next morning. She and her mum stayed close to the phone, waiting for news. The younger twins were sent to friends' houses. The kitchen became the meeting point – neighbours, police, anyone who came to help.

The phone stayed on the table. Every ring made them flinch. Most were calls from neighbours, local reporters called too. At first Janette took every call, then started letting them ring out. There were only so many times she could say the same thing.

***

Witnesses would later remember the small things and detectives used their statements to form the backbone of the early inquiry. Each description placed Vicky in roughly the same spot during the same time frame, narrowing the search area to a few hundred yards between Hopetoun Street and the police station. They said she was memorable for her manners, how she smiled when she spoke.

The driver of the last bus would go on to remember it as an uneventful run. He didn't recall seeing a girl matching her description at the bus stop.

The timetable for that route was checked in full. The final service to Falkirk left Bathgate not long after seven.

All the drivers who worked the shift were interviewed and shown Vicky's photograph. None remembered picking up a girl matching her description. Inspectors went through ticket stubs and route logs, but nothing suggested she boarded any bus that night.

It seemed the trail had run dry and soon the days began to run into each other.

Posters with Vicky's school photo went up in shop windows and bus shelters. Volunteers joined the search, combing the lanes and woodland near the A706. Radio bulletins ran every hour, each one ending with the same line: police were keeping an open mind.

The press moved in. Reporters stood outside the house, waiting for updates. The family kept the curtains closed. Janette barely slept.

As February dragged on, the search grew wider. There were appeals on television and a handful of possible sightings that went nowhere. Hope turned into endurance.

Lothian and Borders Police led the investigation with support from Central Scotland Police. In the early weeks more than a hundred officers were involved. Search teams worked along the Union Canal, through farmland and patches of woodland. Police divers swept sections of the water. Helicopters circled overhead conducting aerial sweeps. Officers went door to door across Bathgate, Redding and Falkirk, checking sheds, outbuildings and roadsides.

The phone lines at Bathgate Police Station never stopped. More than 70 sightings were logged, some from just a few miles away, others from the far end of the country. People were certain they had seen a girl like her in Stirling, Perth, Dundee, even Newcastle. One caller from Aberdeen said she had spoken to a girl at a bus station who fitted the description. Another was sure she had seen Vicky in a cafe near Dundee. Police followed

VICKY

every one of them up. Each sighting meant paperwork, phone calls, and long drives that ended in disappointment.

Most callers meant well. They had read her name in the papers or seen her photo on the evening news and wanted to believe they could help. A few were time wasters or people chasing attention. The detectives treated them all the same. Every report was logged, checked, and passed to the next team to verify.

Inside Bathgate Police Station, detectives did what they could with what little they had. Every day without a lead or trace of Vicky added to the pressure. Each night ended the same way, with more questions than answers.

By early March, the investigation had gone national. Forces across Britain were circulating her photograph and statement sheets. Detectives from other divisions phoned in to compare details and timings. The case had grown too large for one station to manage, yet it still came back to the same point. A 15-year-old girl had vanished from a town centre and no one could say where she had gone.

Police knew they could not keep up the searches – and they would have to scale it back.

The search teams were stood down. The daily sweeps and helicopter runs had done all they could. The inquiry shifted from fieldwork to paperwork. A small core of detectives kept working from Bathgate, checking routes, statements and background leads, but the big operation was over. They still spoke to Janette and Vicky's dad Michael and said they were doing their best. They meant it, but their words began to sound thin.

At home, Janette tried to hold things together. She told friends the police were brilliant and she believed it, because belief was all she had left.

Vicky's smiling face was a familiar sight to the public.

The search would go on but so would the waiting.

For a time, hope sat in the small things for the Hamilton family: the phone ringing late at night, a car slowing outside, an unexpected knock at the door that made everyone stop breathing.

Each one ended the same way. With no news and no Vicky.

***

Eleven days after Vicky disappeared, her purse was found in Edinburgh.

It lay beneath a Portacabin at St Andrew's Square bus station, the main terminal for buses heading south. Inside were her national insurance card, her bus ticket from Livingston to Bathgate and a few coins.

From that point, major newspapers and television networks became interested. Vicky's disappearance featured on BBC *Reporting Scotland*, STV's *Scotland Today* and in every major Scottish paper.

The family made repeated televised appeals, with Janette urging her daughter to come home. Tip-offs came in from all over the country – sightings on buses, in cafes, in shopping centres – but none could be verified.

The purse find was the first real lead the investigation had. Detectives followed it east, convinced it might explain how she

VICKY

had vanished. If she had travelled on to the capital, there was a chance she had gone further.

They spoke to drivers, searched hostels, checked the five buses that left Bathgate for Edinburgh that night. None of the drivers remembered her. No one at the station recalled seeing a schoolgirl alone.

Still, the purse changed the direction of the inquiry. Officers were sent to London on the theory that she might have run away or been taken there.

For weeks they searched stations, hostels and night shelters, talking to anyone who might have seen a Scottish teenager travelling alone. Nothing came of it.

Over those first months Lothian and Borders Police logged more than 7,000 names. Nearly 4,000 statements were taken. Every lead was checked, most of them dead ends. The file filled box after box in the Bathgate incident room.

By summer the investigation into the disappearance of Vicky Hamilton was classed as open but inactive.

Through the rest of the 1990s the case would stay open under the Major Crime Review Team.

New appeals would be issued on every anniversary – the day she was last seen, her birthday, significant years passing such as year one, five, year 10.

Any new leads those appeals generated would be checked, any unidentified remains found in the UK would be cross-checked.

Detectives later confirmed that Vicky's disappearance remained one of the largest missing-person investigations ever handled by Lothian and Borders Police.

Back in Bathgate, life went on. Buses still came and went, and some people walked past the bench without looking twice.

Others couldn't pass that stretch of road without thinking of Vicky. The takeaway where she had sat with her chips, the bench by the window, the pavement outside the police station all became reminders of what had happened. What had once been just another corner of the town carried a different weight after that night.

"That's the last place Vicky Hamilton was seen," they'd point and shake their heads, briefly sad for a child whose picture they had seen on the news or in newspapers and occasionally on police missing posters.

Vicky did nothing wrong. She was cautious and polite. But that counts for nothing when the wrong person crosses your path. The space between one place and another can be enough to lose everything.

In Redding, Vicky's photograph stayed in the window. The Hamiltons carried on because there was no other choice. Janette phoned the station for updates but there was rarely anything new. The police were still looking, they said. Neighbours stopped by with food or flowers, then less often as the months went on. People meant well, but they had their own lives.

Vicky's room stayed the way she had left it. Her schoolbooks were still on the desk, her music cassettes lined up in order. Janette said she could still smell her perfume sometimes, though she wasn't sure if it was real or a memory.

The phone still rang now and then. Most calls were reporters or mistakes. She answered them all the same.

VICKY

Time wore Janette down. She went back to work for a while, trying to fill the hours, but exhaustion showed in her face. Friends said she stopped sleeping, her voice rough from too many cigarettes and tea.

She tried to keep a brave face for the younger children — six-year-old twins Lindsay and Lee — and for Sharon, but the fight was leaving her.

When the second anniversary of Vicky's disappearance came around, she looked years older.

In January 1993 she collapsed at home and was taken to hospital in Falkirk, where she died soon after. She was 41. The official cause of death was heart failure but those who knew her said it was a broken heart waiting for her daughter to come home.

After that, Michael and Sharon carried on the appeals together. They faced the cameras each February, repeating the same words. Someone must know. Please come forward. They spoke with determination, their faces drawn by years of strain.

Each anniversary brought another small piece in the newspapers. Detectives would phone, checking to see if the family had heard anything new. They never had.

Through the 90s, Vicky's case appeared in the lists of Scotland's missing.

And that was where it stood: a missing purse, a false trail to London, and a 15-year-old girl who vanished between two bus stops on a cold February night.

Time moved on in Bathgate, but the memory stayed. The

takeaway changed hands, the bench outside was replaced, yet everyone still knew the story.

A young girl had disappeared and an ordinary evening turned into one of Scotland's longest unanswered cases.

CHAPTER TWO

DINAH

IN THE SUMMER of 1991, fields across the south of England filled with crowds chasing music and freedom. Dinah McNicol was 18, and her life was opening up in front of her.

She had just passed her A-levels, earned a place at Sussex University to study religion and philosophy, and decided to take a year out. She wanted to earn money, travel, and breathe a little before stepping into the next part of her life.

Dinah was tiny, barely 5ft tall. She dressed in headscarves and jumpers from charity shops, dreadlocks tucked behind her ears. She liked to stand out and didn't care who was watching. She was a confident, happy young girl.

At home in Tillingham, Essex, her father Ian tried to let her go without showing his nerves. He had raised five children on his own since his wife Judy died in a car crash when Dinah was just six. Social workers had questioned whether a widower could manage, but he refused to let them split the family. He worked as a chicken farmer by day and played jazz at night to keep the house going. When he had no one to watch the children, he took them with him.

They would sit in the car with crisps and lemonade while he played the saxophone in smoky pubs and village halls.

The McNicol household was chaotic but close and Ian was a good father.

Dinah grew up learning to look after herself, to fight her corner and speak up. She had seen what loss could do, and it made her determined to live life fully.

To friends she was bright, kind, and brave. Music ran through everything – it was the background to her homework, it was the soundtrack to nights spent in Chelmsford Park with pals, passing a cheap bottle of cider and talking about the future. She loved Muddy Waters and Talking Heads, often blasting 'Once in a Lifetime' from her bedroom until the walls vibrated.

She was a thinker, often deep in conversation, but she was fun too – the kind of girl who could make a room feel lighter just by being in it.

At school she stood out for her independence as much as her grades. Teachers labelled her as bright and questioning, someone who thought deeply and spoke her mind. She was close to her siblings but eager to find her own way.

That summer, Dinah worked part-time in local shops and helped her dad with odd jobs around the house. She often talked about the future, saving for travel, maybe moving near the sea once she started university. For a girl from a quiet village, those plans felt enormous. She spoke about them often, not with arrogance but with the certainty she had the drive and confidence to make her dreams happen.

DINAH

However that July, she had begun to feel restless. Essex felt too small, too familiar.

She wanted to see more, to push further, expand her horizons.

When she heard about a free festival called Torpedo Town on Bramshott Common in Hampshire, she decided to go.

She'd never done this kind of thing before and that made it irresistible. Thousands of young people were heading there, drawn by the music and free from the shackles of parents, school and work.

The early 90s were the height of Britain's free-party scene. Convoys of trucks and vans took over disused airfields, commons and quarries, setting up speakers and tents wherever there was space. Police and councils were caught between enforcement and exhaustion. The Criminal Justice and Public Order Bill that would later clamp down on raves was still three years away, so most gatherings ran unchecked. Hampshire Police logged complaints from locals about noise and traffic that weekend, but officers were ordered to monitor from a distance unless violence broke out.

Her father was nervous about her going, but he let her. He told himself she was sensible and could look after herself.

Torpedo Town was rough and loud. What began a few years earlier as a small travellers' gathering had by that day in 1991 become part of the free festival and rave circuit that moved from field to field across the south of England.

Bramshott Common filled with tents and vans, the smell of food, petrol, smoke and sweat mixed together. Music played around the clock, guitars during the day and heavy dance tracks through the night. There were no rules or security, with lots of fires burning and people drinking, talking and dancing until morning. Police kept their distance unless things got out of hand. It was not safe or organised, but it had its own rhythm.

Dinah moved through the festival easily. She was fearless, open to talking to everyone and taking it all in.

And then she met David Tremlett, a 26-year-old from Essex.

He was older, friendly, and she could tell instantly he was harmless. She felt a connection with him and mixed with Tremlett most of the weekend and when it was time to go home they packed up together and decided to look for a lift.

It was Monday, 5 August 1991. They were standing at a petrol station on the A3, trying to hitch a ride. Hitchhiking was still common, especially after festivals when trains were crowded and buses irregular. Roadside lifts were normal among students and travellers. Dozens of young people moved that way every weekend during the summer. It was not seen as reckless, only practical. No one imagined that such a small decision would become a huge risk.

A man pulled in and said he was heading towards Brentwood, not far from Dinah's home. It sounded ideal. The pair got in.

As the car reached the M25, Tremlett began to feel uneasy. As the driver pulled over Tremlett turned to Dinah.

"Get out with me," he urged.

She smiled, staying in the back seat. Tremlett stepped out but he felt very nervous. Something had been off about the driver. He couldn't put his finger on it as he'd been fairly chatty and

DINAH

just an average man. He watched as the car pulled away. Dinah waved to him.

It was the last confirmed sighting of her alive.

***

When Dinah didn't come home that night, her father tried to stay calm. Maybe she was with her grandmother. Maybe she had gone to visit her sister Sarah in London.

But two days passed and there was still no word. Ian went to the local police and reported her missing.

Detectives began tracing her movements from the festival. Witnesses placed her at Bramshott Common and later at the petrol station. Tremlett gave his statement, repeating what he had told friends – that he'd felt uneasy and that Dinah had chosen to stay in the car.

Soon after, her bank card was used across the south coast – in Brighton, Hove, Portslade, Margate and Ramsgate – draining the small compensation money she had received after her mother's death. While the withdrawals gave a false sense of movement, no one had seen her. Detectives traced each withdrawal through the National Westminster network, matching times and camera angles, but none of the cashpoints had CCTV then. Bank staff in Brighton and Margate confirmed the card was used correctly, with the right PIN. That meant whoever made the withdrawals either had her card and code, or she was with them willingly. Without video evidence, the theory remained open. Officers examined the handwriting on her bank forms for possible forgeries, but no clear lead emerged.

For her family, it was torture.

Police followed the trail for weeks, sending officers to Brighton, Hove, and Margate, checking hostels and shelters, showing her photograph around bus and train stations.

Every lead fell flat. The withdrawals of cash both frustrated and perplexed officers.

Ian clung to the hope his daughter was alive and had perhaps gone travelling, too caught up in her newfound freedom to call. But as the days started to turn into weeks, his hope began to thin.

Police cast their net wide. Essex took the first reports, Hampshire traced her last known movements, and Kent checked the banks along the coast. Officers chased every scrap of information – the petrol station, the bank card, the festival crowd – but nothing held. The free-party scene moved on, witnesses vanished, and they couldn't trace the man in the car.

Police appeals went out. Her photograph – young, smiling, dreadlocks tied back – appeared in newspapers and on television.

In pre-internet days, missing-person appeals relied on newspapers, local radio and television bulletins.

The family's appeals were handled by Essex Police's press office, who circulated the same school photograph to every newsroom in Britain. Missing People UK used it again in national campaigns. Reporters described Ian McNicol as calm and articulate but visibly broken. He spoke to newspapers and TV, repeating the same line: "Someone must have seen her. Please, just tell us."

DINAH

Friends and teachers spoke of her warmth, her curiosity, her plans.

There were sightings, of course. Dozens. A girl who looked like her on a ferry. Another in a London café. Another hundreds of miles away in the north east. Each one led nowhere.

The investigation spread but yielded little. There was no body, no crime scene, no witness who had seen what happened after that car pulled away on the A3.

As months passed, the inquiry was merged into the National Missing Persons Bureau database and later recorded into HOLMES, the police information system linking major cases across forces.

In the mid-90s it was formally classed as a long-term missing-person inquiry.

Reviews were carried out every few years by new officers, checking any potential links to unidentified remains or other cases involving young women who disappeared while hitchhiking. Nothing matched.

For years, it remained that way. Ian tried to protect his other children from the worst of it. He kept the routines going as best he could, but the strain showed. His working life became increasingly precarious, and his health suffered. Friends said he seemed overwhelmed at times by the weight of not knowing what had happened to his daughter. In Tillingham people often avoided him, unsure what to say. The silence was worse than their pity. One night he walked into both pubs in the village and told everyone he didn't mind if they spoke to him. It was better than being blanked in the street.

At home he made decisions that hovered between hope and the acceptance she was never coming back. He cleared out Dinah's clothes but kept her books.

He stayed in the same house, waiting. Every time the news mentioned a body found, his heart jolted.

"My heart panics," he described. "When they say it was a boy I feel sad for the parents, but glad it wasn't Dinah. But now I'm getting on a bit, I would like to die knowing where she is and have it finished."

He worked to keep her name alive and in the minds of the public.

In 2004 Dinah's photograph appeared on milk cartons in Iceland supermarkets as part of a campaign for missing people. The picture showed her smiling in a headscarf, bright and unguarded.

"I still dare to hope that one day she'll walk through my door and give me a hug," Ian said.

Then, in May 2006, with all hope abandoned, Ian held a memorial service.

He sang the jazz standard 'Dinah', the song that had given his daughter her name.

His voice trembled, but he sang anyway. He was, he said, trying to think upwards, not downwards, to choose joy where he could. It was his way of surviving what life had taken from him.

His body grew weaker, but he refused to give up. He had suffered ill-health, yet still spoke about his daughter whenever anyone asked. He said he wanted to live long enough to know what had happened. He wanted to bring her home.

DINAH

While Dinah's disappearance might have faded from the headlines, in Ian's mind she was still at the forefront of his thoughts.

The police file sat in storage, revisited now and then by officers who could offer little in the way of anything new. Leads came and went. There were sightings that went nowhere. Police followed tips from the south coast. A girl with dreadlocks seen in Brighton. Another in a flat in Hove. A rumour she had joined travellers. Each sighting collapsed under scrutiny. The photographs were shown around hostels, squats, festivals, but no one knew her name. The bank card had been used, but by who, no one could say.

One officer said it felt as if they were following a ghost.

Ian kept the house the same. He didn't want to pack up her books or lose the chair she used to sit in so everything was kept in its place.

Whenever Ian saw his neighbours, they would ask after her but he never had any new answers. The village noticeboard carried the missing poster long after others had stopped.

Parish newsletters mentioned her anniversaries, and school friends sent Christmas cards to her father every year. It was their way of saying they hadn't forgotten about Dinah.

Outside, the garden grew wild, but he said he liked it that way. It made the place feel alive.

Even after 16 years of waiting, Ian would answer every call hoping one would bring the news he needed even if it was the news he feared the most. Dinah's face stared at him from the photographs pinned above his piano – her smile still the same even as the years moved on without her. In the photo she is 18, clever, curious and certain of her future.

Dinah's name stayed on the national database, a photo among thousands, waiting for the day a match would come and explain what happened to her.

Until then, she remained caught in the summer light of 1991, on the road home.

CHAPTER THREE

ANGELIKA

THE SKY ABOVE Glasgow was grey. It might rain or it might not. You can never tell what way the weather will turn. September in Scotland is unpredictable, it can be blazing sunshine or it can be freezing cold and wet.

Angelika Kluk didn't mind. She was used to erratic weather and the damp cold that seeps through to your bones and doesn't leave.

She pulled on her jumper without thinking about it and planned the day – Sunday, 24 September – ahead.

This was her third summer in Glasgow. She had first come in 2004, then again in 2005, and now, 2006. Each time she stayed longer, always returning to the same place.

When Poland joined the European Union in May 2004, Glasgow saw one of the highest rises in new arrivals from Central Europe outside London. Many came for temporary work in hospitality and construction. For women like Angelika, short-term seasonal jobs in hotels and cleaning firms were easy to find through church contacts or agencies. The Polish community in the west of Scotland grew quickly; by 2006 local newspapers were running stories about Polish food shops opening in every district.

St Patrick's Church – with its red sandstone and Gothic features – was one of the last buildings left from Anderston. Everything else around it had been cleared in the 1960s to make way for the M8. Now the motorway ran almost flush with the church, close enough to feel the vibrations through the stone on a busy day.

But the building was an old familiar in a part of Glasgow that had been gutted and rebuilt.

The church was designed by London architect Peter Paul Pugin and opened in 1898. The sandstone made it look stern and dark from the outside, but inside the details were striking. A white marble altar rested on six dark green columns sent over from Connemara, Ireland. A Caen stone cupola rose above the throne. Stained glass from Birmingham's prestigious Hardman studio caught the light – the same workshop that had produced windows for cathedrals across Britain, including Westminster and St Mary's in Glasgow. It was the kind of craftsmanship that stood out when Anderston was a rough, working-class corner of the city, all shipyards and smoke and in an area where there was more soot than stained glass.

Families lived 10 to a close, many of them Irish, almost all of them Catholic, and every one just trying to stay warm, earn a living, and keep going.

St Patrick's didn't match its surroundings. It wasn't supposed to. The polished marble, the carved capitals, the great east window – they were statements. This was a church built to last and be seen.

By the time Angelika came to Glasgow, Anderston was half-

ANGELIKA

demolished and half-rebuilt. The old Anderston Centre stood mostly empty, a few shops clinging on while the rest waited for demolition.

The area had been crumbling for years. You could still see what it had once been, but 'regeneration' mostly meant flattening what was left.

By the early 2000s the area was changing fast. The Europa Building went up where the bus station once stood, new offices like the Cerium followed, and the Argyle flats came later. The whole thing looked thrown together.

Even so, parts of Anderston kept a strong parish identity.

St Patrick's hosted Polish-language Masses once a month and opened its doors to students and migrant workers looking for cheap rooms. The church house doubled as both presbytery and guest accommodation. It was common for visitors from Poland or Ireland to stay for the summer, doing odd jobs around the grounds in exchange for board.

Angelika liked it there. She loved the church, its people, and she felt welcomed and safe. She'd taken to calling herself Angela because some people struggled with her real name and anyway, she quite liked the anglicised version of her name.

Angelika Kluk was more than a headline or a police file. She was a daughter, a sister, a student. A young woman who carried both ambition and laughter with her into every room.

To understand the true weight of what was lost, you need to know who she was before Glasgow, before St Patrick's and before her name became bound to tragedy. She had come a long way from her roots.

***

Angelika was born in 1983 in Skoczów, a small town in southern Poland with a population of about 25,000.

It sits near the Czech border, where the Beskid mountains stretch low and green across the horizon, and where the Catholic Church still holds much authority.

Skoczów was the kind of town where faith was stitched into everyday life. On the hill known locally as Kaplicówka, stood a chapel and a tall cross honouring St John Sarkander, the town's martyred son whose memory was woven into local faith.

In the 1980s and 1990s, Pope John Paul II was the central figure of Polish Catholic life. His portrait hung in homes and classrooms, and his visits to the region were remembered with pride.

For Angelika and her older sister, Aneta, that devotion wasn't abstract, it was part of their childhood: Mass on Sundays, feast days marked in the calendar, candles lit beneath his image. Easter. Christmas. She wore her first communion dress with pride and found comfort in the ritual of it all.

Later, at university, she joined religious societies and found her voice in small gatherings, but the seed of that religious devotion was planted in her hometown.

Angelika grew up on the third floor of a five-storey block just off the main street. The flat was tiny, two bedrooms, a narrow kitchen, a balcony that looked out over the yard where the neighbours' children played.

She and her sister Aneta shared a room crammed with two single beds and a wardrobe that always seemed too small for their clothes.

ANGELIKA

Their father, Władysław was a construction worker who left early and came home late, his hands rough from working with cement and dust. He cooked simple meals, soup, potatoes, pork cutlets, and kept the girls in line with understated discipline.

After Angelika's parents divorce, Władysław raised the girls alone and was determined to give his daughters a decent start, even when money was tight.

Their school was at the end of the road, a low concrete building that Angelika walked to every day. She wasn't the kind of pupil who drew attention. She wasn't loud or dramatic. Teachers remembered her because she was the opposite: diligent, polite, the kind of student who always handed in her homework, always had her head down in class and never talked back.

"She was studious, very bright, but also a happy girl," one teacher said.

Another remembered her smiling "almost all the time", not in a showy way, but as though she carried an inner calm within her.

At home she read constantly, books borrowed, swapped, and begged for. Languages fascinated her. English especially.

She copied words into a notebook, underlining them, practising the sounds under her breath. For her it wasn't just a school subject. It was a doorway: to music, to films, to conversations she imagined having far beyond Skoczów. Her world might have been small, but her dreams most certainly were not.

When she was born, Poland was still under communist rule so her early childhood was shaped by ration books, state television, and grey housing blocks that lined towns like hers across the country.

But by her teens, the world had shifted.

The old regime was gone. Elections were held. Markets opened. People started to dream beyond their borders.

And in 2004 – her first summer in Glasgow – Poland joined the European Union.

For her generation, the change was huge. Suddenly, they could live, work, and study anywhere in Europe. This meant choice and freedom and she started to believe there were opportunities beyond Poland.

But somewhere between her second and third visits to Scotland, that quiet life began to shift.

When she left Skoczów for the University of Gdańsk, her world widened but her habits hardly changed. The city was bigger, louder, more colourful than anything she had known at home. The streets along the Motława River teemed with students and tourists; the old town's brick churches and Hanseatic facades towered over cafés and bookshops. For most students it was freedom. For Angelika it was a way to move forward, not mess around.

She moved into the student halls like everyone else, but while her classmates filled their nights with vodka-fuelled parties in smoky kitchens, Angelika kept to herself.

She went to her lectures, read in her room, and went home when she could. Her classmates called her "a bit old-fashioned".

According to her friends, she was always neat, always prepared for class and never sloppy.

Her lecturers felt much the same. She was diligent, serious, respectful, not the sort to challenge or coast. Others might scrape through on charm or bravado; Angelika's gift was persistence.

"She always had the notes," one classmate said. "If you missed a lecture, you went to Angelika. She let you copy them. She never refused."

Languages were her way of reaching out. She chose Scandinavian studies, specialising in Norwegian, but it was English that held her heart. For her, language wasn't a chore to be endured, it was a key to the future – a path beyond Skoczów.

Her faith travelled with her too. In Gdańsk she joined small religious groups where the conversation was serious with people she felt comfortable with. It was in those rooms she opened up more than she did elsewhere. She smiled, laughed, shared thoughts she would have kept hidden in class. It was a slow blossoming. She wasn't suddenly outgoing, but she was beginning to find her place.

Angelika was drawn to Glasgow – maybe because her sister was there, maybe because of the people, or maybe the distance from home. Scotland seemed a world away from Poland and she would listen as Aneta told her all about her adventures in Glasgow and the beauty of the country and how welcoming it was for foreigners. Angelika was eager to see it for herself.

Whatever the reason she had for coming to Scotland, something about Glasgow loosened her.

She had travelled before, but Scotland felt different. It was loud, chaotic, and at times grimy yet she liked it.

The Glaswegian habit of talking to strangers, of calling you "hen" or "pal" as though you'd known each other for years, caught her by surprise at first and then it made her feel welcome.

She found work cleaning offices in the morning and then in the afternoon she would work in a hotel – it was long hours, changing sheets, scrubbing bathrooms, stacking laundry and it was exhausting but she never complained. She was used to hard work – she thrived on routine.

Most of the young Poles working in the city at that time held multiple jobs. The Scottish press described them as the "hidden workforce", keeping hotels, bars and office blocks running through the night. Employers valued them for reliability rather than pay.

Angelika fitted that pattern perfectly, disciplined, punctual and determined to save for her studies.

Between her shifts she would return to the chapel house where the atmosphere was closer to a family than a religious workplace. She brewed tea in the kitchen, tidied the sacristy, folded vestments, and set out hymn books. She took pleasure in seeing everything just right. To the parishioners she seemed happiest when she was useful – polishing brass candlesticks, sweeping the floors and lending a hand wherever it was needed.

There were lighter moments too. Trying to teach a parishioner a few words of Polish she laughed when he mangled the sounds. Another she helped in the garden, brushing soil from her hands, hair tied back as she bent over the flowerbeds. She wasn't loud or showy, but she left an impression – polite, thoughtful, steady.

She made friends there, though she kept her private life to

ANGELIKA

herself, warm but reserved. Never dominating a conversation, always listening, always smiling. She kept notebooks close at hand, jotting down English words and turning foreign idioms into neat Polish script.

By her second summer, she felt more at home. She ventured further across Glasgow, exploring cafés and shops, catching the bus into town, lingering in bookshops.

She learned the rhythms of the diocese – when the building would be busy, when it was quiet.

By the third summer, she was no longer a visitor. It was her home from home. She had her own room, her own routines, her own circle of people who noticed if she wasn't around.

Back in Poland she had been reserved, studious, even shy, but in Scotland she started to come out of herself. She made friends, she explored, she became more open, more confident.

The quiet girl who kept to herself in student halls was now learning golf, making new friends, and questioning things she once took for granted and, surprisingly, this included her faith.

Angelika had met Father Gerry Nugent during one of her early visits. She had gone to Mass at St Patrick's and introduced herself afterwards. A few weeks later, when she needed a place to stay, she asked if he knew of anyone with a spare room. He offered her one at the church.

She was, Father Nugent thought, a terrific worker. "She fell into this community," he said. "She told me it felt like home."

But by the summer of 2006, Angelika seemed to have changed again.

She spent more time with older men. One, Sheriff Jim

Forrester, was a senior judge who became a friend. He gave her lifts now and then, she reminded him of his daughter. It was a genuine platonic relationship between a kindly older man and a girl he was fond of.

Another, Martin Macaskill, was a married chauffeur she had met while working for the same Russian family, Angelika as a nanny and Macaskill as a driver.

Her sister Aneta disapproved, believing "she was worth more than that".

But Angelika's diary told a different story. It was filled with references to him, notes of love, confusion, hope, guilt.

"I am horribly, helplessly, blindly in love with him," she wrote.

In one entry, she described drinking tea with him, sitting together in silence.

"For a few seconds," she wrote, "we felt we were the richest people in the world."

Angelika did seem settled. She had friends, routines, and people who cared about her, even if some blurred lines they shouldn't have.

She was due to fly back to Gdańsk on Wednesday, her bag already half packed for home.

On Saturday night, she went to the driving range with Sheriff Jim. He gave her a small gift before dropping her off at St Patrick's. They hugged, and she told him she'd see him next year.

She was rooted in two places now.

The next day's parish diary listed nothing unusual. Sunday Mass, confession, cleaning rota, and choir rehearsal in the evening. Father Nugent's sermons that weekend focused on for-

ANGELIKA

giveness and trust. Nothing about the church suggested trouble. Parishioners came and went, unaware that the last hours of a young woman's life were unfolding behind the heavy wooden doors.

***

On Sunday, 24 September, Angelika went to Mass as usual, smiling and greeting familiar faces.

Back in the kitchen she made herself tea and toast. Her notebook lay open on the table beside her, lines of English handwritten in tiny print. Father Nugent passed through the kitchen and she greeted him softly. He nodded, distracted and she returned to her notes.

Later, she fetched a mop from the vestry cupboard and cleaned the tiled floor near the sacristy. She wiped the brass edges of the candleholders and arranged the hymn books by height, as she always did. A few parishioners passed through. One asked if she wanted a hand; she smiled and said no, she was nearly done.

At around 2pm, she took a break outside, sitting on the wall near the garden shed. She had a sandwich wrapped in foil and a small bottle of juice. She watched the road for a while. A bus passed. She didn't wave.

She spent the day texting Martin. It was ordinary and normal.

Later, someone saw her near the shed with a paintbrush. She might have been touching something up, or helping someone. The details blurred in hindsight. But she was smiling.

That was the last time anyone remembered seeing her.

Around 3pm, as residents of William Street were settling into their Sunday routines. The EastEnders omnibus played on televisions. Outside, the air was mild, windows open, voices carrying down the street.

Several neighbours heard a woman's screams – screams of terror – sharp, panicked, high-pitched. It was not drunken laughter or a couple quarrelling, it was a woman and she sounded desperate. One said it was the worst sound he had ever heard – so awful it made him freeze. He went to the window but saw nothing. The noise stopped abruptly, replaced by a silence that seemed even more chilling.

Just beforehand, Martin received Angelika's text, telling him she loved him. This would be the last message she ever sent.

Later that night he called. No answer. He tried again a few minutes later. Still nothing. The calls went to voicemail. No ring, no click. Just the line, then her answering machine voice, then the beep.

At first, he told himself it was nothing. She might be out, her phone could be on silent, she might be in the shower, or with someone, or just not checking it. But as the minutes dragged into hours, that excuse began to wear thin.

Unease settled in his chest. He tried again. Still no answer. He drove across the city, checking places they had been together, familiar routes, the quiet spots they'd park up in the car. He returned to the church, looking for signs she might be inside. Nothing. No sign of her.

By midnight, he was frantic. He called again and again. Straight to voicemail.

ANGELIKA

Back at the chapel house, her room was untouched. Her bed was neatly made. Clothes folded. Her bag where she had left it. Everything in its place – except Angelika.

By Monday morning it couldn't be ignored. Angelika had disappeared.

Her belongings hadn't moved. Her phone was still off. No one had seen her since Sunday afternoon. Martin, his wife and Aneta went looking for Angelika. Father Nugent was not involved in the search.

The mood in the house had changed. People moved quietly, opening doors, calling her name, checking places that didn't need checking, double checking rooms they'd already looked in.

Maybe she had fallen and hurt herself, maybe she couldn't call out, they thought. They searched and re-searched until it was clear Angelika had vanished into thin air.

Martin went to the police and told them he hadn't heard from Angelika since Sunday afternoon. He looked exhausted, his hands clasped together on the table. He said he'd been calling her phone since the day before but she hadn't answered.

When the officers asked how he knew her, he hesitated. Then he said it – they were in a relationship. He was married, he admitted, and he knew how that sounded. But he said he cared about her, he just wanted to find her.

It wasn't the kind of confession the police hear every day – a man admitting to an affair with a missing woman – but it certainly got their attention.

A missing persons inquiry was opened. Officers visited the church and began taking statements.

They looked through her room, made notes, and asked the standard routine questions. Had anyone seen her? Had she left the building? Was there any reason she might stay away?

They canvassed the area. Strathclyde Police opened a formal investigation within a day. That kind of urgency was unusual, but the circumstances were too. Officers sealed off the church grounds, began door-to-door checks, and logged every call connected to Angelika's phone.

Detectives used the HOLMES 2 system to track witness statements and cross-reference timelines. Forensics were notified, though no scene had yet been identified.

Neighbours were asked if they had seen anything unusual. A few mentioned hearing a scream – high-pitched, sharp, not drunken shouting or arguing – though no one could pinpoint when it had happened or where it came from. The account was noted.

At that stage, it was just another detail in a growing list of uncertainties.

Angelika was on the cusp of everything. Her degree lay ahead, her career, her relationships, her future. Glasgow was meant to be a chapter in that story – a season abroad before returning to Poland with sharper English and wider horizons.

That is why her disappearance cut so deeply.

To lose Angelika was not to lose a statistic. It was to lose a young woman whose life was still unfolding. She should have gone home with stories of a Scottish summer, of friends made, of a new language learned.

Instead, her story was about to end – suddenly and brutally – on an ordinary Sunday afternoon.

ANGELIKA

The police acted quickly. Quicker than most missing person cases. Angelika wasn't the kind of girl who went off for a weekend or forgot to call home.

Her sister said it wasn't like her. The people at the church said the same. So did a sheriff.

Sheriff Jim had seen her the night before. He told police she'd seemed happy and relaxed. He was a respected figure, not someone easily dismissed, and when he raised concerns, officers listened.

The calls came from the church and from Martin, almost at the same time. By the time police arrived at St Patrick's, they already knew this wasn't a routine inquiry.

By Tuesday morning, the story had spread. Early editions of the *Evening Times* carried a small item on page five: "Concern for Missing Student."

That afternoon, national broadcasters were running live reports from outside the church. Strathclyde Police confirmed a full investigation.

The first official press release described Angelika as "slim, 5ft 3in, with brown hair and brown eyes, last seen wearing jeans and a jumper." It was standard wording, but it made the case real. Reporters were already outside St Patrick's, camera crews waiting for updates.

Some parishioners gathered to pray for her, others just stood around, not knowing what to say.

At Cowcaddens police station, Angelika's sister Aneta faced the press. She stood in front of the cameras, pale and tired, and asked for help.

"She wouldn't just disappear," she said. "Something has happened."

Her words were simple but they cut through the noise. This wasn't just a missing student anymore. This was a sister, a daughter, a woman far from home and now possibly in danger.

Aneta lived in Glasgow and knew how careful her sister was. If Angelika wasn't answering calls, something was very wrong.

Back at St Patrick's, the police presence was growing. Detectives went in and out of the chapel house. They took statements, collected items, and began treating the building as the centre of the search.

By the end of that day, the posters were up. Angelika's photograph showed a young woman with a soft, open face. It was hard to connect that image to the fear that had taken hold of everyone who knew her. Her photograph showed a smiling young woman.

Within hours, the image was everywhere – news bulletins, web headlines, front pages. Polish-language stations in Glasgow rebroadcast the appeal, translating Aneta's words for families watching back home.

At the Polish Social and Educational Society hall in Kelvingrove, parishioners gathered to light candles beneath her photograph. Journalists noted how quickly the city took her to heart; she had become 'everyone's daughter, everyone's sister'.

Parishioners gathered to offer their help. Some volunteered to search nearby parks and rivers. The story was spreading fast and the chapel community was bonding together.

For Angelika's family in Skoczów, it was agony. They had spoken to her just days earlier.

ANGELIKA

Now she was missing in a foreign city, and her sister was appealing for help on her behalf, thousands of miles from home.

That first week set the tone for what followed: intense, uneasy, filled with rumours that spread faster than facts. Reporters crowded the pavement outside St Patrick's, filing updates between police briefings.

Inside, detectives worked in near silence, piecing together the last known movements of a girl who had come to Glasgow for study, faith, and belonging and had vanished in the very place she should've been safest.

CHAPTER FOUR

A DRIFTER CALLED PAT

In the summer of 2006 a man calling himself Pat McLaughlin turned up at the Loaves and Fishes group in Glasgow.

Denis and Cathy Curran had built their charity around feeding and supporting the homeless, and Pat seemed like he belonged there. He looked like a man who had learnt to keep his head down. He was polite, carried little more than a bag of clothes and seemed tired.

He ate quietly, thanked them, and left. Just one of the thousands they had seen pass through their door.

Loaves and Fishes had started years earlier in a church hall on Glasgow's southside, born out of the Currans' belief that nobody should go hungry in a city as wealthy as Glasgow.

They handed out soup and rolls from the back of a van, no questions asked.

In 2006, the charity's base shifted between several parish halls, St Simon's, St Alphonsus', and St Mary's among them, wherever space could be found for a few hours each night. The Currans' van was a familiar sight on Glasgow's streets, its folding tables set up under bridges or near the Clyde. Regulars queued for soup and tea, tradesmen dropped off loaves from local bakeries, and volunteers came from every denomination. It was a small, stubborn network of people who refused to turn a blind eye to poverty and to people down on their luck.

What began as a few volunteers soon became a lifeline for people sleeping rough or struggling to get by. It was never just about the food. The Currans treated everyone who came through the door like a person, not a problem to be fixed.

They remembered the names and the faces. The next day Pat came back. Men like him came and went all the time. Some stayed a night, some a week, some tried to get clean, others didn't. The Currans treated them all the same.

Pat fitted the pattern they were used to seeing – polite, sometimes quiet, always grateful.

Later police would learn that Tobin often inserted himself into places exactly like this – church kitchens, homeless shelters, community halls. He knew how to act humble. He never pushed to the front, never caused trouble. He waited to be invited in. Patience made him disappear into the background. There was nothing in him to hint at danger.

He offered to help stack chairs and sweep floors. They accepted it as it was something useful he could do.

Loaves and Fishes fed whoever turned up, not just men who slept rough but women trying to keep warm and the long-term homeless who moved from one shelter to another.

St Patrick's Church was also part of that loose network of places that helped. Word travelled fast that often a bed could be found at the chapel house too.

Before long, Pat appeared at St Patrick's.

He walked there from the city centre, carrying a holdall and a few tools. The volunteers thought he had come through word of mouth.

At that time St Patrick's often took referrals from Loaves and Fishes, so nobody questioned it. He said little about himself, only that he needed work and somewhere to sleep. The chapel house side entrance led straight to the basement, and that became his territory.

Father Gerry Nugent had always opened his doors to those with nowhere else to go, and the parish was used to drifters passing through. Pat offered to paint fences, shift rubbish and tidy the chapel garden. He kept his head down and worked steadily.

To the other volunteers he was unremarkable, quiet, sometimes courteous and sometimes sullen.

But there were the small moments that unsettled people – a curse when a tool broke, a door slam that made people look up. One parishioner felt he stared at her for too long, another that he could change suddenly from friendly to withdrawn. But they reasoned he'd had a hard time, he was homeless, transient, who knew what horrors he'd seen on the streets. He was, after all, just another man passing through.

St Patrick's itself was a warren of rooms and half-lit corridors which he moved through easily. He stored the paint tins in the basement, smoked at the side door and sometimes slept on a mattress near the boiler room. When the church emptied at night, he was still there. Pat had a way of blending in until he was barely noticeable.

The basement was cluttered with broken pews, tins of paint,

old hymnals stacked in boxes. Few people went down there unless something needed to be fixed. It was an easy place for a man to disappear.

In Brighton he had done odd jobs for a parish. In Worthing he swept paths. In Portsmouth a priest had found him handy but intense. In Margate he had been the quiet man who knew where the tools were kept. He was almost always somewhere near a church, always close to people who trusted first and asked questions later.

He'd had many names during his time on the streets of Britain, 'Pat McLaughlin' was just the latest mask. Churches gave him what he needed: a roof, a meal, a reason to be there. Priests rarely asked questions. Parishioners assumed goodwill. Pat understood that. He knew when to lower his eyes, sound grateful and make kindness work in his favour.

At St Patrick's he blended into the rhythm of the place. He carried hymn books, scraped moss from the steps and tidied the corners others ignored. He never explained who he was or where he came from, and no one asked.

The parish house at that time was busy with volunteers, clergy, and foreign students who came and went daily. In that constant movement Pat found cover. He could be helpful without being noticed, useful without being known.

Angelika Kluk saw him often that September, passing him in corridors and courtyards as she went about her own work. To her he was simply Pat, one more face in a church full of transients. He called her his "little apprentice".

At the time, no one at St Patrick's could have guessed that the man living in the boiler room was not who he said he was. The name, the story, even the accent were part of an old routine.

He had lived like this for years, hiding behind new names, pretending to have faiths, slipping in and out of people's lives without leaving a trace.

Only later would they learn the truth.

Pat McLaughlin didn't exist.

The name traced back to a false identity card he'd once used before.

It had served its purpose then; it served him again in Glasgow. By the time anyone looked closely, the man using it had already vanished and the truth behind it had taken another life.

As the name Pat McLaughlin vanished, another surfaced. That was how he had lived for decades, always a few steps ahead of anyone who might ask who he really was. He used whatever name suited him at the time. Sometimes it was Peter Wilson, sometimes James Kelly, sometimes one he spotted in a newspaper or thought up on a bus. He kept his stories simple. He was a handyman, a painter, a man down on his luck. He would work for a while, then move on, leaving nothing behind. Brighton, Portsmouth, Bathgate, Margate, each just another stop on a long road.

It seems obvious now, the false names, the rent books written in his shaky handwriting, the sudden disappearances. But Britain in the seventies and eighties was an easy place to vanish. Records sat in filing cabinets that nobody opened unless they had to. Local police forces guarded their own patch and rarely spoke to the next county. A Peter Wilson in Brighton had nothing to do with a Pat McLaughlin in Glasgow. He thrived in those gaps and built a life between them.

His real name, Peter Tobin, was banished into a history few remembered.

CHAPTER FIVE

THE MAN WHO LEARNED TO VANISH

PETER TOBIN WAS born on 27 August 1946 in Johnstone, Renfrewshire, and grew up in Shettleston, Glasgow. He was the youngest of eight children. His parents had more mouths to feed than money coming in. It was a bleak time. Glasgow was still recovering from the war, the air thick with smoke and soot from the shipyards and foundries.

Rationing might have ended, but poverty had not. Families were crammed into tenements where neighbours heard every cough, argument, and radio broadcast across the landings. The Tobins lived as many did, on the cusp of hardship. His father worked when he could, often on the trams or in labouring jobs. Working or not, he spent too much of his time and the family money on drink. His mother cleaned for other families and kept her faith as her only comfort. Sunday Mass was never optional for the children. She scrubbed their shoes and sent them to church even if they had nothing else that was clean to wear. It was a small act of dignity in a life that offered little else.

Shettleston in the 1950s was a working-class district plagued by poverty and poor health. The city was trying to modernise but was still scarred by bomb damage and industry decline. Rows of blackened tenements stood shoulder to shoulder along narrow streets. It was crowded but close-knit, a place where everyone knew each other's business. Smoke from the yards mixed with winter fog, turning the sky a permanent grey. Green trams rattled past, carrying workers to the docks and families to the city centre.

Children made the streets their playground. They chalked out hopscotch squares, played peever and kick-the-can, and rolled marbles they called booles. In some streets, the council even closed the roads so they could play safely. Denbeck Street was one of them, known locally as a Play Street. Families might have lived on top of one another in flats where space was scarce and sound carried through every wall and even though privacy was rare, community still ran deep. The post-war years brought small signs of change. New housing schemes like Sandyhills were built on the city's edge, replacing the worst of the slums. The council talked about better living, but the old problems of smog, overcrowding, and poor health didn't disappear. Shettleston remained the kind of place where people worked hard, looked out for each other, and got on with life.

Tobin was seen as a restless child. Teachers thought him bright enough when he wanted to be but could not sit still. He talked back, skipped lessons, and liked the attention that came with his defiance – even if that attention was a rap across the knuckles.

By seven he had been sent to a reform school, an institution meant to straighten out difficult boys. Reform school in the 1950s was sold as a second chance. For most boys, it was a warning that came too early in their lives to mean anything. The buildings were cold and stern, more punishment than education. The days began before dawn. A whistle blew, sharp and final, followed by the scrape of regulation boots on bare floorboards.

Each boy was given the same uniform when he arrived: a coarse grey shirt, short trousers that itched at the knees, and heavy lace-up boots, often a size too big. The laces were stiff, the collars starched, and nothing ever quite fit.

The boys would line up in silence, washed in cold water from metal basins fixed to the wall, and dried their hands on thin towels that never did the job. The school smelled of soap, boiled cabbage, and carbolic. Then it was time for chapel. The benches were narrow, the prayers long, and the only sound was the echo of the warden's shoes on the flagstones. Breakfast followed and this was typically porridge ladled into tin bowls. The boys were ordered to eat quickly and no talking was allowed. After that came work.

Some boys were sent to the workshops to learn carpentry or shoe repair. Others were marched outside to dig or paint fences until their hands blistered. Talking back brought a beating; slow work brought solitary confinement. The days were ruled by clocks and whistles, and by the end of the week most of the children would be miserable. Every hour was accounted for.

The staff said it was good discipline for naughty boys and believed the structure would turn bad boys good. In reality, it taught them how to become tougher and survive. Tobin learned to spot weaknesses, he would flatter the officers and stay quiet when tempers rose. Boys who fought were broken by it. Boys who bent the rules learned how to work them. Tobin learned that pretending to be sorry was safer than being sorry. Scotland had hundreds of boys like him – poor rather than wicked. A theft born of hunger, a fight that went too far, a father missing or drunk. Most were out again within a year, older but not wiser. The country called it rehabilitation. By the time they left, most had learned the only one thing: never show what you feel and never let anyone see you angry.

Borstal came next. Tobin was sent around age 15. It was supposed to be the last step before real prison, a place where work and order would set young men straight. The system was the same, only harsher. Uniforms, drills, forced labour, and endless inspections. Those who kept quiet and behaved earned their release and those who challenged authority would be kept longer. Tobin kept quiet. He learned that charm and obedience could open doors faster than any temper could.

When he finally walked out, whatever softness had survived childhood was gone. He had learned how to play the system and how to wear a mask. He knew that a lie got you further than the truth. It was a lesson that would serve him for life. When Tobin was released from borstal before his 18th birthday the Glasgow he had left two years before had changed.

The shipyards were still going, but the work wasn't steady or regular. Men would clock in for a few weeks and then they would be laid off. The pubs filled earlier, the talk darker and more bitter about lack of work and lack of money. There was a feeling that the best years had gone, though nobody said it out loud. Men drank to forget there was no work in the morning and the irony of spending money they didn't have on drink was lost on them in their misery. The government had announced they would redevelop some areas. Old tenements were pulled down and families scattered to new estates on the city's edges, Easterhouse, Drumchapel, Pollok. They were meant to be fresh starts but many schemes were built too far from where the jobs were. The sense of community that had once held districts together began to fade.

It was a hard, masculine world where violence was prevalent. A slight in the pub could end in a fight in the street. Tobin fitted easily into that crowd. He worked when there was labouring to be had, slept where he could, and spent his pay as fast as he earned it. Quick with his hands, quicker with his temper, he became part of the violence that filled the city's back lanes. In those years, a man could vanish inside Glasgow itself. Cheap lodgings for single workers lined the streets, old houses divided into rooms, dark basements, church hostels. Nobody asked for references. Cash was enough. Tenants came and went with the shifts. It suited Tobin. He could charm a landlady until the lies began to fray, then move on before the rent came due.

The pattern of his life was set: short stays, sudden exits, no roots. The law barely noticed him except when he crossed it. Burglary, assault, petty theft, nothing remarkable in a city where half the young men had records by 20. But for Tobin, it became a habit. The system was too crowded to track one restless man, and he learned to use that to his advantage.

THE MAN WHO LEARNED TO VANISH

When he looked south, it wasn't ambition that pulled him but instinct. England meant distance. New towns, new pubs, new names. A chance to start again without his past following him down every street. The journey south was easy then. You could buy a cheap rail ticket, step on a train in the morning, and vanish into a new life by nighttime.

He arrived in Brighton with a holdall and a story at the ready. There were always rooms to let near the sea, boarding houses run by people who wanted cash and asked no questions. Tobin always seemed to be able to suss out the houses run by women, usually widows. He was polite, called them "missus," and offered to mend a door or paint a wall for an extra week before payment. It was a routine he would repeat for years.

Brighton had once been grand, but by the early 1970s its glamour was fading. The hotels were peeling, the pier lights flickered, and the tourists who had once filled the promenade were going abroad for real sunshine. The town was left to students, pensioners, and drifters. On the side streets off the seafront, men queued for labouring work that might last a day or two. Tobin blended into that crowd. He told people he was a painter, sometimes a handyman, always between jobs. He kept his tools in an old canvas bag and spoke little about where he'd come from. He learned that confidence could pass for respectability.

From Brighton he went to Portsmouth, taking rooms near the docks. The city was full of noise and drink, a mix of sailors, labourers, and men running from something. The pubs opened at 11 and stayed busy all day. He could disappear there without effort. He worked odd jobs near the naval base, left behind half-finished repairs, a pile of cigarette ends, and unpaid bills.

Worthing came next. Smaller, quieter, a town of retired couples and tired hotels. He stayed in a room above a shop for a few weeks, kept to himself, and moved on before the questions started. As one neighbour said, he was "polite enough, but something was off". Nobody could say what that something was.

In Eastbourne he found a few days' work painting a small hotel near the seafront. The manager saw him as polite and distant, the kind of man who didn't joke with others or stay after hours. He never gave an address and collected his pay in cash. By the time they thought to ask where he'd gone, he had already disappeared.

Margate came after that. He rented a terraced house with a small shed out back and told neighbours he was a decorator. Some remembered the smell of paint drifting through open windows, others the sound of a radio late at night. He offered to fix gates, repair steps, and clear gutters. Friendly enough, but something about him kept people at arm's length. One neighbour remembered he would vanish for days and then return as if nothing had happened.

Each move was a repeat of the one before, a short stay, a burst of charm, then he was gone. Paint tins, cigarette ends, unpaid rent. He was living on the margins, where records were written in pencil and forgotten as soon as the page turned. Britain's seaside towns were full of men like him, renting rooms by the week under names nobody checked.

Religion gave him another disguise. Churches offered food, warmth, and people willing to believe in redemption. He used that faith as cover. In Brighton he went to Mass. In Portsmouth he joined evening prayers. In Worthing he swept the yard of a Baptist mission and told the minister he was trying to find his faith again. He learned when to bow his head, when to look penitent, when to hold a silence long enough to seem sincere.

He did the jobs that made him useful. Painting fences, cleaning halls, carrying boxes of food to the back door. The staff liked him, they said he was mild and helpful, the sort of man who fetched chairs without being asked. They wanted to believe he was a lost soul worth saving. He looked humble enough to pass for honest.

For Tobin, places of worship meant food, warmth, and an easy network of trust. Churches didn't run background checks or share information. They saw people in need, not risk. Each new parish was a clean slate, every priest another chance to build a false history.

He played the part until suspicion crept in. When someone asked too many questions, he moved on. There was always another shelter, another church, another charity needing a man with a paintbrush and a story about redemption.

The country made it easy. Police forces still worked within their own borders. A man could change his name, cross a county line, and become someone else. Even when arrested – in the early days this was for property crimes such as theft and housebreakings – it often meant only a few weeks or months before release. The cycle repeated.

By the 1980s, computer systems like HOLMES were being developed to link information across forces, but they came too late. He was already years ahead, living in a world of paper records and half-forgotten names.

By the mid-1980s he was heading north again. The jobs had dried up and there were debts he didn't want followed. Bathgate offered anonymity. Neighbours heard arguments through the walls then nothing.

The rent was unpaid, the room stripped bare and no way of tracing the tenants. For his whole life the pattern never changed. Debts left behind, hurting the women he supposedly loved, neighbours relieved to see him go. Each new address was a clean slate, each alias another escape. On their own, each trace looked ordinary. A tenant who moved on, a worker who couldn't settle. Together they formed a trail of harm, a record of a man who learned how to slip through the cracks and stay there. Tobin wasn't clever in the way of masterminds. He was clever in the way of parasites, knowing exactly how much to take before moving on. He survived by being half-seen and half-remembered, never long enough for the truth to catch him up. You may wonder how a man like that could vanish for decades. The truth is, he didn't. He simply learned that most people look away from what unsettles them. Peter Tobin learned to disappear in plain sight, and the world let him.

CHAPTER SIX

THE BODY IN THE CHURCH

THE DAY LOOKED warmer than it felt. It was a clear autumn day in Glasgow but with a slight chill in the air. The sunlight was sharp enough to make you squint. There had been rain earlier so the pavements were glittering from the sun bouncing onto them. The air smelled of wet stone and petrol from the nearby M8 motorway.

Two days earlier, on Thursday 29 September, police had found the body of a woman under the floor of St Patrick's sacristy. They had been searching the church for days, crawling through its narrow corridors and storerooms, looking for anything that might explain Angelika's disappearance. A detective had noticed something that didn't sit right, a pew pushed slightly out of line, the scrape marks on the boards where it had been moved. When they shifted it aside, the floor looked uneven. They prised up one edge and the air that rose was stale and heavy, carrying the smell of rot and damp wood.

The space beneath was barely high enough for a child to crawl through. The boards had been laid thick over old stone foundations. When the first beam of light hit the darkness below, they saw a shape wrapped in plastic sheeting. At first it looked like discarded materials, maybe tools or leftover timber from repairs. Then someone saw the curve of a hand, small and pale, and everything stopped. For a few moments nobody spoke. Every person in the room understood what they were looking at.

One of the first to go below was a scenes of crime officer from Strathclyde Police. He lay flat on his stomach and eased himself into the gap. It was so narrow he could barely turn his head.

Dust drifted with every movement, stinging his eyes. He inched forward using his elbows, cutting carefully through the layers of plastic. The light from his torch bounced off the wood and soil, the air thickening with heat and decay.

He stayed under there for more than two hours. When he finally crawled out, grey with dust and sweat, he pulled off his gloves and said only that it was her. They had found Angelika Kluk.

A few hours later, another expert entered the crawl space. Forensic scientist Carol Rodgers made the decision herself. She had been called to assess the scene and ordered that the body remain untouched until she could take samples with her own hands. Lying flat, she eased her way beneath the floorboards, the same narrow tunnel the scenes of crime officer had just come through. The air was heavy and close, the heat from the lamps pressing against her back. She worked methodically, scraping, swabbing, recording, each movement slow and precise. When she finally emerged, her overalls were grey with dust and her face drawn with exhaustion. Those who saw her that night spoke of her calm, of how she never flinched. It was not bravado. It was professionalism, the kind that demands a person go where nobody else can.

The first detectives who saw the scene described it as one of the worst they had encountered. The narrow space, the compressed air, the nearness of the church walls, it felt wrong in a way that words couldn't express. One officer said it was as if the building itself were holding its breath.

Forensic teams took over the vestry and worked through the night, marking out every inch. Samples were taken from the boards, from the soil beneath, from the layers of sheeting and tape that covered her. Each fragment was photographed, labelled, and passed up through the hatch. Nothing was hurried. Every movement was measured and deliberate.

Outside, floodlights threw long blue shadows across the sandstone. The street was sealed off and the low hum of generators filled the air as reporters gathered behind the tape. Parishioners who came to leave flowers were turned away. One older woman crossed herself and stood at the gate for a long time, tears on her face, refusing to leave.

Inside, the forensic photographer worked in near silence. Each lift of a board had to be recorded, each trace brushed away, labelled, and stored. The smell of disinfectant mixed with the damp air from the crawl space until it clung to every surface.

In the hours after dawn, officers moved the body out of the narrow vault beneath the sacristy floor. The space was too tight for a standard stretcher, so a rigid board was slid in and the remains were drawn out slowly. Witnesses would later remember the silence of the police officers, the soft creak of wood under weight and the click of cameras in the dim light.

When police confirmed that the body under the floor was Angelika, Father Nugent was told. He went very quiet, bowed his head and, holding the small crucifix he kept in his pocket, said a short prayer. It was not loud or ceremonial, just a few words for her soul. He stayed in the presbytery for a while after that, sitting on one of the chairs with his hands folded, staring at the floor.

The team had sealed the space and replaced the boards. They logged the last entries in their notebooks and packed up their gear. The lights were switched off one by one until only the weak glow of morning filtered through the stained glass. Dust hung in the coloured beams, and the air tasted of disinfectant and smoke from the floodlights outside. The church felt hollow, stripped of its purpose.

Over the next two days, specialists returned again and again. They scraped beneath the new boards, searching for missed fragments, and swabbed for traces of blood, hair, and fibres. A forensic anthropologist studied the notes and photographs, marking how she had been left, her body twisted, the plastic pulled tight. It showed haste, not care. Whoever placed her there had been desperate, frightened, certain only that he needed her hidden.

Outside, more people gathered at the edge of the tape, bringing flowers, candles, and rosary beads. Someone fastened a photograph of Angelika to the gate, her arm around her sister, both of them smiling. By mid-morning the railings were bright with colour against the dark stone.

At Pitt Street headquarters, detectives briefed the press. They confirmed that a body had been found but refused to name her. Reporters didn't need them to. Glasgow already knew.

That night, a forensic van left the church, escorted by an unmarked car. It drove along Anderston Quay and onto the expressway toward the mortuary at the Southern General Hospital. Inside, the pathologist waited with her team. The body of Angelika Kluk had been underground for almost five days.

When the van reached the mortuary, the staff worked in silence as the plastic was unwrapped layer by layer. Forensic pathologist Dr Marjorie Turner dictated her notes in a low voice, each detail recorded without hesitation: the bindings, the tape, the marks. It was a grim routine but essential. They worked through the smell and the heat, professional and steady, every note preserving another piece of the truth that would later be told in court.

The investigation was moving fast. Detectives now had a body, a name, and a missing handyman who had disappeared days earlier. The search widened by the hour. Cars were traced, lodgings checked, and photographs circulated between police forces across the country. The name Peter Tobin was beginning to surface off the record as Pat's true identity, not yet public but spoken among reporters who found his name related to a serious sexual assault in England years before and recognised the pattern of how these cases unfolded.

By early evening the church was sealed again. Floodlights still glowed against the stained glass, and a light drizzle had begun to fall. By Friday morning the gossip had started. It was the only story being spoken about in Glasgow newsrooms... As a reporter working in the city at the time, the sordid developments in Angelika's case soon made their way to my desk.

***

Usually on a Saturday, unless I was working away either somewhere else in the UK or abroad, I would be in the office. Although I was hired as an Edinburgh reporter, Saturday's would be spent in Glasgow at our head office in Central Quay. A typical Saturday for me would be filing stories from my car or phoning in stories to the copytakers - telephonists who could type at the speed of lightning while we dictated our words down the line. Saturday's could either be very quiet or extremely busy but that Saturday was strange for me. I had done all my work required for the *Sunday Mail*.

My pages were clean, my deadlines met, and I was stuck at my desk restless and bored. Brendan McGinty, my news editor, knew it. He had me tidying up live pieces, writing fillers and sidebars to sit beside the bigger stories. It was the sort of job you did to fill the hours, waiting for something to break. We were all watching developments from Anderston. The daily papers had the story but the detail was thin purely because of the limited information coming their way. We needed something solid for the Sunday edition, something that would hold.

Working weekends in the news was always a strange balance. Sometimes you prayed nothing big would happen because your front page splash was already nailed down and you didn't want to lose it. Other times you longed for something to break. We used to joke about the nightmare scenario, a royal death at 6pm on a Saturday night, the newsroom half-empty, phones ringing, presses waiting. None of us wished for tragedy, but that was the job. When disaster struck, you were expected to run toward it.

My phone rang. The voice on the other end was familiar. It was a police contact from the old Strathclyde force, someone I had known long enough to recognise the tone that meant something big. Scotland still had eight regional forces then, each with its own way of dealing with the press. In Glasgow, you learned quickly who would talk and who would not. Those relationships were built face to face, not over email or social media. You earned them one story at a time. That night all the usual channels were silent – officers had been told not to speak to anyone. The silence itself told a story, but some people still talked. The voice on the phone was low and cautious.

"A detective spotted a pew out of place," he said. "That's how they found her. They lifted the boards and she was underneath. We know who did it. The handyman's gone."

It was the first time anyone outside the investigation had heard that detail about the pew. That small moment, the thing that looked wrong, would become the line every paper used. I remember sitting back and taking a breath. None of it was a surprise.

Everyone in the newsroom knew Angelika was likely dead, but nobody imagined she had been under the church floor the whole time. I would like to say I was shocked, but I wasn't. You come to stop expecting surprises in this line of work. What I felt was sadness for her, for her family, and for everyone who had trusted that church as a place of safety.

There was no time to dwell on it. I had a job to do. I went straight to Brendan. He didn't waste words. He asked the only question a good editor would've asked.

"Are you sure about your source?"

I said yes, as sure as I could be. He studied my face for a moment and nodded.

"Get a snapper and get down there. Marion will run it from here."

That last part stung. Marion Scott was a senior, well-respected journalist who had been at the paper for years. She was already in the office and it made sense she would write the main piece while I fed her everything from the ground. Still, it burned. The tip was mine. The line about the pew was mine. I could already see how the page would look on Sunday with her byline in bold and mine tucked inside. That was the job when you were still considered a rookie by their standards. You had no choice but to swallow it and carry on.

Photographer Alan Simpson was sent with me. He was a veteran, very funny, good company on long shifts and sharp. We drove across the city with rain smearing the windscreen and the blue flash of police lights ahead of us. Police vans lined the kerb and forensic officers moved in and out through the side door, their heads down, their white suits ghostlike in the light. We said our greetings to the assembled press pack and found a spot where we could observe the comings and goings.

There was no press conference and no official statement.

Every detail had to be pulled from contacts, parishioners or what you could see with your own eyes. Nobody confirmed who the body was. They didn't have to though, everyone there already knew.

We stayed outside for more than 12 hours, the press line quiet but constant. Someone was always on the phone, talking to news desks, copytakers, or police contacts. It wasn't the frenzy television likes to show. It was more casual, respectful but professional. We all knew what had happened inside, and none of us wanted to shout about it.

Every few minutes someone would step away to file a short update or grab a smoke before the next round of calls. The cold crept in as the light faded. We watched the comings and goings of police, the white-suited forensics carrying out boxes, the detectives ducking under the tape. Members of the public came and went too, laying flowers and candles at the gates. When they left, we read the cards and sometimes used their words in our copy. It was the only human touch we had to use that day.

The news editors were hoping Angelika's family, or at least her sister, might appear at the church. They didn't, but the clergy did. A few priests came out to speak with mourners. They asked the reporters to be respectful and keep their distance, which we did. They were tight-lipped about everything else. Father Gerry was nowhere to be seen. As the day wore on and news spread, the flowers multiplied, forming a patchwork of colour. The smell of lilies and candle wax clung to the railings. The city felt different: subdued but not indifferent. Glasgow has a way of closing ranks around tragedy, and people came because they needed to bear witness.

The next morning *The Sunday Mail* ran my story on the front page. The pew detail. The missing handyman. The sealed church and the grieving parishioners at the gates. Marion Scott's name sat above it; mine ran inside. I remember reading it early that morning and feeling a strange detachment. The words were clean, the layout perfect, but they looked distant, stripped of the noise and exhaustion that had gone into getting them. I was proud of it, but felt hollow too. For the paper the story was finished, for that day at least. For Angelika's family, it was only the beginning. The focus had shifted again. Police were searching the country for Peter Tobin. Every newsroom in Britain was chasing him now. I didn't know it then, but that weekend outside St Patrick's would mark the start of something that would follow me for years.

CHAPTER SEVEN

THE MAN BEHIND THE NAME

THE WEEKEND HAD ended, but the story hadn't. I tried to switch off. In all likelihood, I thought, by the time I went back to work on Tuesday, the story would be over. I assumed he would be found and charged and we wouldn't be able to write anything more until a trial took place.

At that point, I felt my involvement in the Angelika Kluk murder was over.

The news was running in the background, the usual hum of voices I wasn't really listening to. Then I heard the words that pulled me back in.

A man had been found in a London hospital after taking an overdose. It was 4 October 2006.

They didn't name him at first, just hinted that it was connected to a murder in Glasgow. The church murder. But within the hour, the confirmation came. His name was Peter Tobin.

He'd checked himself into the National Hospital for Neurology and Neurosurgery under the name James Kelly. Another alias and one he'd used many times before.

He was alive, and detectives from Strathclyde were already heading south. It was a strange kind of relief. If he'd been found dead, the story would have ended there, another unanswered murder, another family left with half the truth. But he was breathing, and he could talk, his attempt at suicide had failed. Back in the office the next day, the mood in the newsroom was the same as always. Everyone was chasing their own deadlines. Unless it was war or royalty, no-one really cared about what anyone else was working on.

But for me, that was it. I was now the Tobin reporter. As phones rang in the background, chairs scraped and the hum of the newsroom continued, my energy changed from routine to urgent. I was now chasing every scrap of detail I could find about Peter Tobin.

At first, his name meant nothing to anyone. Then his old records began to surface.

He had a history of violence. He had seriously sexually assaulted two teenage girls in England. Assaults stretching back decades. The picture grew darker with every new fact.

He had called himself Pat McLaughlin in Glasgow, but his real name was Peter Britton Tobin. The details were coming piece by piece: false names, fake addresses, years spent moving between towns. As I'm sure every reporter working on this story did, I began calling old police contacts and at the same time police trawled through their files. Two sides of the same coin but with different goals. What they and what we found wasn't just a man with a violent past, it was a man who had lived his whole life telling a lie. Each day brought a new revelation. He had been married three times. There were women who'd fled him and his violence. He had served time in prison for multiple offences, the worst being rape. The more I learned, the clearer it became that Angelika wasn't the start of his story. She was where it finally ended. Some of the blanks we were able to fill from old court reports.

In May 1994, Peter Tobin pleaded guilty at Winchester Crown Court to raping one 14-year-old girl and sexually assaulting another. The attacks had taken place nine months earlier in his flat in Havant, near Portsmouth. He had offered the girls cider laced with drugs and both collapsed. One later regained consciousness, and managed to escape into the street, half-dressed and disorientated, where she raised the alarm.

Inside the flat, the second girl was left badly injured and unconscious. {Check with lawyer we can say this about his son} Tobin's young son was also present that night and walked into the room after the assault, interrupting what was happening. Cathy would later be told that his presence may have prevented the attacks from going further.

By the time police forced entry to the flat, Tobin had already fled. Officers found the second girl hidden in the bathroom, bruised and barely breathing. There were traces of the drug Tobin had used, blood at the scene, and clear evidence of violent sexual assault. Tobin disappeared and remained on the run for several weeks before he was traced and arrested.

The judge at Winchester Crown Court sentenced Tobin to 14 years in prison and he served 10.

When he got out in 2004, he moved north to Paisley. He kept

to the same old pattern: new town, new job, new name. The neighbours would later say he was a quiet man.

In October 2005 he attacked a 24-year-old woman in his flat in Johnstone, near Paisley. She had gone there thinking she could trust him but he was already on the sex offenders' register.

The attack came suddenly. One minute he was calm, the next he had a knife in his hand. She fought him off, caught the blade, and felt the skin split across her palm. He lunged again and she twisted free and ran, barefoot, blood running down her arm.

She made it into the street and banged on a neighbour's door. When the police came she was shaking and bleeding. They took her statement, sent her to hospital, and promised to check the flat. But they waited until the next day and when they finally turned up, he was gone. They never explained why they waited until morning. The official line was that officers attended "as soon as practicable". It was a glib phrase that covered a failure. The woman had turned up bleeding and terrified, but the urgency didn't seem to reach anyone.

By the time they walked through the door, Tobin had stripped the place. The bed was bare, the cupboards were empty. There were faint bloodstains on the floor and a knife missing from the kitchen block. They took photographs, logged the scene, and issued a warrant. It was never circulated nationally and that failure would later haunt the investigation. If the alert had reached other forces, his name might have been picked up before he ever set foot in St Patrick's.

Months later, after his conviction, the woman he attacked spoke publicly, describing him as calm one second and raging the next. She said the part that haunted her most wasn't the knife or the blood, but the knowledge that if the police had acted faster, Angelika might still be alive. Her words were truthful, not bitter, and they cut through the official statements and excuses. She was right.

For months after that attack, Tobin drifted through the south of England, using false names, picking up casual work, sleeping in hostels and B&Bs. He was well practised at hiding without drawing suspicion.

It's a mystery what drew him back to Scotland, but by the summer of 2006 he was there again. He met Father Gerry Nugent who gave him odd jobs and a place to sleep. It was an act of kindness Tobin knew how to exploit.

***

By the time detectives reached London after his overdose, he was stable but barely speaking. The hospital ward was quiet except for the hum of the monitors. Strathclyde officers stood by his bed, waiting for him to open his eyes. When they read him his rights, he barely reacted. Later, under escort, he was taken north to Glasgow, cuffed and flanked by detectives who already suspected that this man's story reached far beyond one church.

The story had changed shape. It was no longer about a murdered woman. It was about a man who had hidden in plain sight.

By the end of that week the Crown Office had authorised

charges. On 7 October 2006, Peter Tobin was formally accused of the murder of Angelika Kluk.

Things went quiet after that. The cameras packed up, the church stayed behind tape, the flowers at the gates began to wilt. It looked finished from the outside, another murder case wrapped up. But it didn't feel finished. Not to me.

The city felt subdued in the days that followed. In cafés and bus queues, people spoke in shocked tones about the church handyman with the false name. Callers to radio shows wanted to know how a man with a record like his could have worked in a church. The disbelief was mixed with anger. Glasgow is a city that prides itself on knowing its own, and Tobin had slipped through that net.

Something about him, the way he had moved through places, the aliases, the years that didn't add up, made it hard to believe this was the full story. Every instinct I had told me that men like him didn't just start at 50 or 60. They learned those habits early. They practised them.

Behind the scenes, senior officers were already asking the same questions. Who was this man really? Where else had he lived? What else had he done? Those questions would become the start of an investigation that would stretch far beyond Glasgow.

I didn't know it then, but finding him was only the beginning. His name would open doors to cases long buried, and the real story of Peter Britton Tobin was still waiting in the dark.

CHAPTER EIGHT

FIRST WIVES – FIRST WARNINGS

TUESDAYS WERE ALWAYS quiet for a Sunday newspaper, the weekend rush had passed and the next edition still felt far away. This was the day for pitching stories to the News Editor, checking out what was likely to come up that week and maybe just chasing down any tips. Woe betide any reporter who didn't have a story to pitch on a Tuesday – even if it meant by Saturday your fantastic 1,500 word double page spread had been reduced to a 200 word page 55 sidebar story.

As was often the case – as I'd been hired as an East of Scotland reporter – I wasn't in Glasgow that morning. I'd planned to work from our Edinburgh office, though "office" was putting it kindly. It was a few rooms in a shared block near Fountainbridge, tucked between other small businesses and the smell of the brewery that still drifted through the air. The carpets were worn, the lighting wasn't great, and the heating only worked when it felt like it. It wasn't terrible but it wasn't great. The only thing it had going for it was there was a car park which meant we could safely park our cars outside the office without worrying about a ticket – and we could get out on jobs faster.

Before that, we'd had decent offices in Castle Street. Big windows with spectacular views of Edinburgh Castle. But no car park. Anyone who has been to Edinburgh will know that even in the early 2000s parking was still at a premium and expensive.

But still, the move to Fountainbridge felt like a downgrade in every sense.

There were fewer of us by then too. Both the *Daily Record* and *The Sunday Mail* had suffered redundancies.

At the time, The *Daily Record* and *Sunday Mail* were owned by Media Scotland – part of the Trinity Mirror Group. Alan Rennie was the Editor of the *Sunday Mail*. Circulation was falling across the board for every newspaper across the UK. Advertising was drying up.

The Sunday Mail was still Scotland's biggest-selling paper then, shifting more than half a million copies every week and read by close to two million people. It felt like everyone's Sunday read – our biggest rivals being *News of The World*.

It wasn't unusual to see the familiar red masthead with the white Lion Rampant tucked under arms coming out of church or the pub.

Everyone was talking about "digital strategy" but nobody really knew what that meant yet.

I was part of a new wave of reporters – the future, they said. A 'rising star' of the company. It felt more like an advertising slogan rather than an attempt to encourage strong journalism.

And for people who had been around a lot longer than me,

the industry was starting to feel jumpy, like something solid had begun to crack. Despite my 'newness' at the job even I began to feel the change.

Cuts had been biting for a while. Reporters were expected to do more with less, travel further, file quicker. We all felt the pressure, though none of us admitted it out loud. Not in the newsroom in earshot of the bosses anyway.

Although a front-page splash still meant everything, you could sense a monumental shift was coming and the old swagger of print was just beginning to fade.

But despite this early downturn, in 2006, while Sky might have been filling the airwaves with rolling breaking news, print still ruled.

A solid front page carried weight with the public. The internet was gaining traction, but people trusted what they could hold in their hands. The paper was their proof and we had yet to experience what people now call 'fake news'.

YouTube had only just appeared the year before and it consisted mostly of home videos and shaky clips that took forever to load. Facebook had opened to the public that autumn. Twitter had barely been invented. News websites were basic, refreshed once or twice a day if you were lucky. There were no hashtags, no online debates, no true-crime sleuths. If a story broke, readers waited for the paper or the six o'clock news. The idea that people would one day get headlines on their phones sounded ridiculous. We still filed from hotel fax machines and Nokias. Laptops were heavy, the broadband patchy, and social media was something no one could explain. Journalism was still alcohol, cigarettes and lots of coffee. Back then, a newspaper's front page could still stop a room. People bought it and read it over breakfast or a pint and whatever was printed carried the weight of truth.

That Tuesday morning I was supposed to chase follow-ups from the weekend, pitch a few ideas, maybe make a couple of calls. Nothing urgent. I was blissfully unaware that within hours I'd be heading down south on a story that would take over my life for months.

I was still at home when the call came and Brendan's voice was brisk, the way it always was when something big had broken.

"Tobin's been lifted as you know," he said. "Pack a bag. You're going down south. I want you to get his ex-wives."

I knew we couldn't print anything until much later, after the court case, but I didn't need any persuading. I threw clothes into a case and was on the road to the airport within the hour. Alan Simpson was going with me. Our only brief was to find and secure interviews with the wives of Peter Tobin. Failure was unthinkable. My notebook sat on my lap with his name scrawled across the top page. Peter Tobin.

The radio still carried scraps of the story. A missing student. A handyman in custody. No one yet understood what it would become.

By the time we reached Portsmouth it was late in the day and the air smelled faintly of the sea. When you travel from city to city, you stop seeing the places themselves, you're not there as a tourist, you're there to work. I couldn't tell you if Portsmouth is a nice city or not, I don't remember that kind of detail. I was too focused on the job at hand – tunnel vision if you like.

The houses were large Victorian villas, well kept but weathered. Cathy Wilson, Tobin's third wife, lived in one of them. She wasn't home when we arrived which stressed me out, I knew it would mean hours on the doorstep waiting, possibly aggravating neighbours, maybe a visit from the local police. It had happened a few times before.

Earlier that year I'd doorstepped a Hollywood superstar at her London home and ended up waiting half the day for her to appear. Our presence in the car hadn't gone unnoticed and her neighbours, both well-known British actors, came out to ask who we were and what we were doing. We refused to say, and they threatened to call the police, which they did. The officers arrived, saw our press cards and told them we had every right to be there. The neighbours weren't amused and when the actress finally showed up, she was perfectly polite but sent me on my way.

In Portsmouth, my instructions were simple – stay put and keep an eye on the house. I wrote a note and put it through her letterbox. I can't remember exactly what I wrote, only that it said something along the lines of having come down from Scotland to speak with her and who I was.

At some point later she called me. She'd received the note and asked me to come back at a later date.

That Tuesday evening was the start of everything that followed. I couldn't know it then, but that single knock was the start of a trail of wives and lies that had been buried for years.

A few days later I was standing at another doorway, still in Portsmouth. The front door opened only partway, her hand on the frame and her body angled to block the view. A polite voice, an even politer apology.

"I'm sorry. I can't talk to you. I've already signed a contract with *The Sun*."

The house belonged to Sylvia Jefferies, Tobin's second wife. Not today, then.

No slammed door, no shouting, just a firm refusal. Someone else had her story, and I wished it had been me.

I rang Brendan. He wasn't happy we'd missed Sylvia, but he was a long-time newspaperman. He knew everyone in the Scottish media was chasing this story and it was a guarantee that we would lose some of it, maybe even all. It wasn't my fault we'd been too late. If I thought his understanding at losing Sylvia was acceptance at possibly losing the others, I was soon brought back to earth.

"Find the other wife," he said. "Get to her before anyone else does."

Alan said nothing as we walked back to the car. The camera bag went on the back seat. He knew the pressure I was under.

We'd only been on the road a few days, though it already felt longer. We'd flown south at the start of the week and hadn't stopped since. I missed my 15 and 12-year-old children, but the pull of the job was stronger at that moment. Curiosity, competition, the need to be first — it kept me going.

Our on-the-road conversations came in bursts, then dropped into long stretches of silence.

"He's too old for Angelika to be his first," Alan said, eyes fixed on the road. "Men like that don't start killing at 60."

I nodded.

"There's talk he could be a serial killer," I said. "Cops think there's no way she's the first. But they're only looking at Angelika for now."

Alan nodded. "There'll be more, I'd bet my house on it."

We caught a flight back to Scotland and within hours were heading north again. Another lead. Another door. Rain hit the windscreen, the wipers keeping time. It matched my mood.

MARGARET

By the time we arrived in the Scottish Highlands, the sky was low and the fields seemed to go on forever. The village we were heading for was the kind of place where everyone knows your name and gossip travels faster than the post.

The farmhouse sat a little back from the road, whitewashed and worn by the weather. A few chickens moved around the yard and a washing line lifted in the wind. From the outside it looked ordinary enough.

Inside was a woman who'd been trying to rebuild her life since she was 17.

Margaret Mountney opened the door. She looked tired, and not just from lack of sleep.

I was surprised when she smiled widely at me after I'd introduced myself and it put me on the backfoot as I was used to doors slamming in my face, angry words ringing in my ears.

Mercifully not this day. She showed us into the kitchen and put the kettle on. The room smelled of damp clothes and coffee and a scrubbed wooden table sat in the middle, dominating the room, comfy armchairs surrounded one side of it.

I was still working out how to start, how to pitch it, while Alan sat down, resting his camera on his knee and saying nothing. I told her again who I was and why I was there.

Doorstep conversations were always rushed. Names, papers and reasons blurred together for the person you were trying to reach.

I thought maybe she had misheard and assumed we were looking for a room or to buy eggs or something like that.

She told me to sit down at the table, so I did.

Margaret stayed standing, her shoulders a little slumped.

"I've been expecting you," she said.

I must have looked surprised because she added, "Not you, a reporter, any reporter. Ever since I saw his name and face on the telly, I've been waiting for the knock on my door."

I remember feeling very sorry for her at that moment but I couldn't get my words out before she said, "He was a monster when I was married to him. I'm not surprised."

I could sense the floodgates were about to break so I opened my notebook and said nothing. Margaret sat down and started to speak.

She told me she was 17 when she met Tobin. She was living at home in Glasgow then and working as a typist, but she had big dreams: a teenager who wanted more than what was expected of her.

It was the late 1960s, when girls her age were pushed towards a narrow path: leave school, find a job, marry, have children.

She said she had always felt restless, like she was waiting for something to happen.

Then Tobin appeared. He wasn't from her area and that made him stand out. He had confidence and charm, the kind that drew you in before you realised it was happening and he told her she was beautiful. It was enough to hook her. Within a year they were married. She was 18, he was 22. The wedding was small, just family and a few friends. Her dress was borrowed, her shoes were too small, and the photographs that remain show a young girl who had no idea what was ahead of her.

After the wedding they lived in Shettleston, but soon moved to Brighton.

She told me that the journey south felt more like a kidnapping than a new start. He wouldn't let her tell her parents or family.

Once there, he cut her off completely and would not let her write to her parents or call them. Whenever he stole from a job, they packed up and moved again. She said she was frightened all the time but did not know how to get away.

The change in him was quick. What she first saw as protectiveness became control. He took the keys when he went out, locking her inside the flat. He told her she belonged to him. If she questioned him, he hit her. If she cried, he mocked her. She said he carried a knife and used it to threaten her, telling her that if she did not behave, he would stab her.

She tried to keep the peace by staying quiet, cooking meals carefully, hoping that would help. It never did. If the food was wrong he would throw the plate or smash it against the wall. She remembered scraping potatoes and gravy from the cupboard doors, shaking while he sat in silence. The silence, she said, was worse than shouting.

Neighbours heard the rows but nobody came. In those days, what happened in a marriage stayed behind closed doors. Women were told to manage, police were not called.

One night he beat her so badly that blood ran through the floorboards into the rooms below. Someone knocked at the door but she could not answer.

"I just sat there," she said, twisting a tissue in her hands. "If I opened my mouth, he would have known I had told."

Her eyes filled as she spoke. After all those years her hands still shook. Some things the body never forgets.

The assaults became routine. Even after the attack that nearly killed her, she was too terrified to go to the police.

"I was too damn scared," she said.

Her escape came by chance. The police picked them up in Brighton for something unrelated, said to have been a burglary and forgery offence committed by Tobin, and brought them back to Glasgow.

"It was because of the police that I got away from him," she said. "He was left in the cells and I was allowed out."

She built a life from there. She worked where she could, moved often, then eventually settled back in Scotland. She divorced him in 1971 then remarried and ran a small guest house in the Highlands with her husband, Robert. She said she liked the routine of it, the ordinary rhythm of guests coming and going. But the past stayed close. Loud voices in the street still made her heart race and the sound of keys turning in a lock could take her right back.

When she saw his face again, years later, she knew him instantly.

It was 2006, and his name was on every screen in the country.

"It didn't surprise me," she said. "I knew what he was."

We sat at her kitchen table. The kettle had just boiled and she poured the tea with hands that trembled slightly. As she spoke, she drifted back through the years, to the locked doors, the smashed plates, the words that cut deeper than the bruises. She talked about the night of the blood, the knock she ignored, the footsteps fading outside the door.

Then she cried and apologised for it. Alan worked quietly with his camera and I kept my pen moving and tried not to look at the clock. There is a point in some interviews when the room becomes a kind of confessional, and your job is to hold it steady.

"I thought he would kill me," she said. "Every night I thought it might be the last."

Before I left, she told me about the puppy. He had bought it for her while she was trapped in the Shettleston flat, a small dog she called Bute. It had been her only company when he locked her in. One day it was gone. When she asked where it was, he told her not to worry. Later she found out he had chopped its head off and thrown it from the window.

She said she lost control, that she screamed at him and hit him, and that was when he turned on her. He ripped off her clothes, held a serrated knife to her, and raped her.

She spoke in a quiet voice, almost as if the words might still reach him somehow.

When we left Margaret's house, neither of us said much. I closed my notebook and sat with it on my lap.

I called Brendan as soon as I could and told him everything – the bruises, the blood through the ceiling, the beheaded puppy, the locked doors, all of it. He listened, then said he'd speak to Alan Rennie and Jim Wilson, the deputy editor and ask if they wanted the story. He sounded sceptical.

I didn't blame him, I knew it was a hard sell. It sounded extreme, almost unbelievable, but I was conflicted. I'd been there in the room with her, I'd seen her hands shaking, and heard her voice catch. I think I sowed a little doubt in their minds because, if I'm honest, I wasn't sure I believed her myself.

I agonised about it with Alan. He wasn't a writer, but he was a seasoned photographer with far more years of experience than me listening to people's stories. I'd been a reporter for just under a decade but still felt like a rookie most days.

Alan said he wasn't sure either. Parts of it rang true, but it was the blood through the ceiling that threw us. And a puppy with its head cut off? We couldn't get our heads around it. How could someone lose that much blood and still be alive?

I wanted to believe her and I wondered if maybe she'd embellished parts of it. There would be no confirming the things she said because she'd already told me she didn't report the beatings, the sexual assaults to the police or the dog.

I felt sick waiting for Brendan to ring me but the final decision wasn't mine.

Brendan called me back. "We're not going to do her story," he said. "We just don't believe it all". Editor's decision is final.

It's one I've regretted ever since.

I didn't push hard enough to make them see that maybe she'd overegged it a little but the truth is I should have fought harder to make her story be heard.

I waged an internal battle with myself – I had sat at her table and watched her hands shake, her voice tremble and saw her tears fall. I did not doubt what she was telling me but then the inner voice was saying, 'but you did doubt her and you said so to Brendan.'

When Tobin was finally convicted, she spoke publicly. Everything she told the papers was exactly what she had told me in that kitchen a year before. The flat in Shettleston, the knife, the puppy she had called Bute. Every word of it was true. I'm glad someone took a chance on her because her story deserved to be told.

Margaret died in 2020, eight years after being diagnosed with lung cancer. I never saw her again after that day in Dingwall.

But some stories stay with you whether they're printed or not.

SYLVIA

Sylvia Jeffries had already said no to me but when her public words did come they filled in the blanks her face had given away. The pattern of Tobin's behaviour repeated. Different town, same man.

Brighton in the early 70s looked like a cheerful beachtown

on the surface. The promenade was crowded with day-trippers, the smell of salt and vinegar hung in the air, and the arcades clattered with coins and laughter. Students rented cheap rooms with horrible carpets and talked about changing the world over bottles of warm wine.

From the outside it felt like freedom, but the same old expectations still ruled. You worked, you married, you had children, and you kept up appearances.

Sylvia met Peter Tobin in Brighton in 1973.

She was a nurse in her early 30s, living alone and working shifts, and she'd always thought of herself as capable, sensible, someone who could look after herself. Tobin arrived in her life suddenly, full of charm and confidence.

He was younger but carried himself like a man who knew what he was doing.

He told her she was beautiful, he said he admired women who worked hard. He made her laugh and it felt nice to be noticed.

They married within weeks. It wasn't a big affair, just a small ceremony in Brighton. She wore a simple dress, and in the photographs she looks hopeful but tense, her smile polite.

"When I married him, I married him out of fear," she would say years later. "I didn't think far enough ahead of what he would do once I was married to him."

At first, she tried to make the marriage work. She wanted a quiet life, a home, and a family. She already had a young son, Ian, and she hoped Tobin might take to him, and that they could be a proper family. For a time it looked possible, then it changed and the affection turned to control, the control to violence. He wanted to know where she went, who she spoke to, what she did. He made her account for every minute.

When she became pregnant again, she thought maybe it would settle him. Their daughter, Clare, was born not long after, but she lived only two days. "Breathing problems," the doctors said.

"She was beautiful," Sylvia said. "Tiny, perfect, and gone before we had a chance to know her."

She said she came home from the hospital with empty arms and the sound of other people's babies still ringing in her ears. She folded the baby's clothes and tucked them away in a drawer.

Tobin showed no emotion.

"He told me to stop crying," she said. "He said I was making a fuss. That's when I realised I was completely alone."

The violence grew worse. He would strangle her until her vision dimmed, then let go and walk away as though nothing had happened.

"You have flashbacks," she said. "Lying on the bed with him, with his arms around your throat. He's just pure evil. Absolute evil."

When he lost his temper, he didn't just lash out at her. The family dog had been a gift from him, a small, friendly animal that followed her everywhere. When it barked or tried to climb onto her lap, Tobin would shout at it and throw it out of the way.

"He started ill-treating it," Sylvia said. "He shouted at it, swinging it around by its lead, and I'm thinking, uh-oh."

One day the dog disappeared. He told her not to ask questions and she didn't, she said she already knew what that meant.

"That's when I knew, if he could do that to something innocent, he could do it to me."

The house became a prison. He carried knives and liked her to see them. He threatened to kill her if she ever tried to leave. She'd wait for the key in the door each night, not knowing which version of him would come home. The fear never eased.

"I used to tell Ian to stay very quiet," she said. "If Ian cried or the dog barked, he'd lose his temper. I spent every day trying to keep everything still."

She planned her escape for months without letting herself think about it too much. Her chance came one afternoon when Tobin went out to collect his wages. She packed two carrier bags, one with clothes for her, one for Ian, and walked out.

"I knew I had to get away or he would have killed me," she said. "I left with nothing."

She didn't stop walking.

"I was terrified Pete would come after me," she said. "For a long time, I felt like I was always looking over my shoulder."

It was the 1970s. There were no women's refuges nearby, no laws that recognised domestic abuse, and no one to tell her that leaving was the right thing to do. She didn't go to the police, it just wasn't something women did – because usually they would be told to keep the peace with their husbands, make their marriage work and stay quiet.

In time, she built another life, found work, moved, remarried and tried to create something ordinary after years of fear. But the past never left her completely. Like Margaret, loud voices made her stomach turn and the sound of keys in a lock could stop her in her tracks. She said she still woke at night with the feel of his hands around her throat and it would make her gasp. But she never stopped being grateful for the moment she walked out of that flat.

Decades later she saw his face flash up on the television. The name came first, then the picture. He was older, greyer, but the eyes were the same.

"I knew it was him. I always knew what he was."

Her son, Ian, died years later. She never said how. She only said that losing him brought everything back – the fear, the grief, the years she'd spent surviving one day at a time.

***

Two women, only a few years apart. One barely out of childhood, the other a grown woman with a job and her own mind. They never met, yet their stories showed behaviour that followed the same shape. It began with charm and ended in fear. Control turned to violence. If the dinner wasn't right, the plate would hit the wall. Neighbours heard it but said nothing and both women knew nobody was coming. Back then, you were told to keep quiet and carry on. Their stories were almost the same, different towns but the same man. The warning signs were there, but they weren't recognised for what they were at the time. Alan and I talked about it in the car.

"He's been doing this for decades," he said.

He was right. Angelika could never have been first. Margaret and Sylvia had already lived the early chapters. Perhaps when he was just honing his craft, how to manipulate and how to not only physically abuse women but also subject them to terrifying mental abuse too.

Back at my desk I typed Margaret's account again. I kept it plain, no adjectives doing the work, just what she'd said. The same response came back. Too extreme. Unbelievable.

I still hear that and it sits under this chapter like a low note. An abused woman tried to put a hand on the scale, and we brushed it off.

There are things about that week I've never forgotten.

Margaret's voice stayed low the whole time, even when it cracked. The kettle boiled twice because neither of us noticed it the first time. When I reached to switch it off, she apologised. That's what abuse does, it makes women apologise when there's nothing to be sorry for.

I remember her hands twisting a tissue until it fell apart, but she never raised her voice. The words came quietly, each one landing harder because of that. Alan took a few photographs and then lowered his camera, he didn't have to say why, he knew when enough was enough.

When I later read Sylvia's account, the details were different but the tone was the same. I hadn't been there, but I could see it. The small flat, the crying baby, the air that must have felt heavy with fear and oppression. The sound of plates breaking, the silence after. The dog that didn't survive.

None of this sits easily, and it shouldn't. These aren't stories you shake off when the piece is filed, they stay with you – the voices, the women who told you what happened when nobody else would listen.

FIRST WIVES – FIRST WARNINGS

It would be easy to blame the time. In the 60s and 70s, women were expected to keep quiet and carry on. Violence at home wasn't treated as a crime; it was called a "domestic". Police turned up, told the husband to calm down, and drove off again. Neighbours shut their curtains, priests told wives to pray for patience, doctors patched up cuts and bruises and didn't ask how they happened. The system saw the bruises as family business.

All of that's true, but it still doesn't explain why a man like Tobin was allowed to keep doing what he did. The press weren't separate from that world, we lived in it like everyone else and in the 2000s, papers turned the other cheek, too. Domestic violence wasn't news unless someone ended up dead. It was seen as private business, something for the family to sort out behind closed doors.

Even by 2006, not much had changed. We covered 'domestics' only if there was a court case or something that made it stand out – a name, a headline, a hook that sold papers. The rest never made it past the newsdesk. If a man hit his wife, it was called "a row that got out of hand" and nobody asked what else he had done or how many times it had happened.

We did not know about Tobin then, none of us did. When Angelika was murdered and his name finally came out, we tore through every lead and every old file, trying to piece together a man who had hidden in plain sight. I still think about the women who came first. We did not overlook them, we just did not know they were there. The danger had been building for years and none of us saw it until it was too late.

When I think about it now, I know we couldn't have seen it

then. There was no trail to follow, no-one was talking about a man moving from town to town leaving wreckages behind him. Margaret and Sylvia weren't part of any investigation, they were just two women trying to survive and couldn't tell what was happening to them. Their stories were there, waiting but we just didn't know what they were pointing to.

Alan and I kept moving and my notebooks filled with names and addresses. Glasgow. Brighton. Worthing. Margate… each line was another piece of a life we were still trying to understand.

Every town had someone who remembered him – a landlord, a neighbour, a woman who'd seen him on the stairs and felt uneasy without knowing why.

We stopped for coffee on those long drives, motorways that all looked the same and blended into one. The chat between us got shorter. There wasn't much to say, the facts were heavy enough.

This chapter is not about what he did to strangers in dark places. This is about what he did at home in daylight. It shows what he was when no one watched.

First wives. First warnings. Two young women married him and barely got out alive. Years later they told us what he had done. We listened, but we had no way of knowing how far it went. I think of them when I write about Angelika, Vicky, and Dinah. Their stories began long before anyone was watching.

He did not start at 60….

CHAPTER NINE

CATHY

I WENT BACK a few hours after she called me. As I walked towards her door, I told Alan to stay in the car. I didn't feel much, just the usual knot in my stomach that came with jobs like this. When a story mattered, you shut everything else down. All I could think was don't screw it up.

I knew I had to make it work, there would be hell to pay if I didn't, a steward's inquiry back at the office. We had already lost Sylvia to *The Sun* and Margaret's story was spiked by the bosses.

It sounds cold but that was how it was in that world. A race against time, rival reporters, big money and big names. You had to stay sharp, be top of your game and falling behind wasn't an option. Last meant failure.

I walked up the path and tried to look calm. The note I'd pushed through the door had done its job, she'd called and said I could come back.

I only knocked once before she opened the door.

Cathy Wilson. Tobin's third wife.

For a second we just looked at each other. She had the kind

of face that told you she'd been through hell and made it out. Strong, but nervous underneath. Like someone who'd seen a ghost and in all honesty she really had literally just seen one.

I introduced myself in person this time.

"You came back," she said.

"I did."

Her voice was steady, polite. She stood aside and let me in. She was smiling, friendly but tense.

Inside was tidy, I commented how beautiful her home was. The smell of polish, a trace of cigarette smoke. A framed photo of a boy on the wall. She asked if I wanted tea. I said yes. It was ice breaker chit chat.

We sat at the table and I tried not to stare as she talked a bit about the weather, about how quiet the street was, how I'd travelled a long way. Small talk that didn't matter much. She was thinking about what to say next, and I was giving her space. That was how I worked, I never rushed people.

Then she looked at me properly.

"You want to talk about Peter."

I said I did.

She gave a small nod and was silent as she thought about what to say next. I waited.

"It's a lot to take in. But I knew this day would come. I knew one day he would come back into our lives."

I nodded, I didn't need to say anything.

"He's a monster. That poor girl and her family. I can't stop thinking about them."

The conversation turned to Angelika for a bit — she wanted

CATHY

to know what I knew about it. Usually I'd be guarded in what I said but Cathy deserved to know it all. After all, I was asking her to spill her whole life with him, secrets and painful revelations she probably wanted to stay buried forever. I wasn't here as a counsellor or a friend – I had a job to do and that job was simple: get her to talk to me.

"Alright then. You'd better switch that on."

I put the recorder between us and the tape started to turn. That was how it began.

She started slowly, like someone testing the water. I had no idea of the horrors I would hear that day. She talked for hours and the story came out in sections, slow at first, then faster. She wanted to empty it out, to put it somewhere else.

I sat opposite her and let her speak. I'd learned over the years that people open up when you give them space. You don't need any tricks, you just need to listen.

Alan was snapping away quietly in the background as we spoke.

She met him in Brighton around 1986 when she was 16 and thought she was a grown up. Her mother had died when she was eight and her grandparents had brought her up. They were kind, steady people, but she said she'd wanted her own life and independence had felt like freedom.

Then came Peter Tobin. Older, confident, twice her age. He had a flat near the sea and spoke as if he owned it. He said he had money, a job, a good future ahead of him and she believed him, she had no reason not to.

Later she would find out it was all false. The flat came with his job. The job didn't last. He didn't own a thing, not even the lies he told.

The flat was in Kemptown, one of those faded terraces that sat between the main road and the sea. From the outside it looked respectable enough, a tall Victorian house split into narrow rooms and cheap flats. Paint flaked from the iron railings, the front step was worn smooth by years of tenants coming and going. You could hear the gulls from inside, that thin, harsh sound that never stopped. When the wind changed you could smell salt and petrol drifting in from the pier.

It was a one-bedroom place, small and square. The kitchen looked onto the back of another house, where washing lines crossed the back garden. The carpet was thin, the wallpaper bubbled where the damp pushed through and a single gas heater kept the chill off in winter. It wasn't squalid, just temporary, a stop-gap sort of place. You got the sense that everyone in the building was waiting to move on to something better.

Tobin told Cathy he owned it and said it was theirs, a fresh start, security. She believed him. It was the first real home she had shared with anyone since her grandparents' house. He said he worked in maintenance for a local property firm, that he was trusted, that people relied on him. The truth was the flat came with the job, the rent was tied to his work, and when he lost it, they would have to leave.

She said she used to sit at the window, looking at the street below, watching people walk to the shops or the beach. She told herself she was lucky but then he started closing the curtains in the afternoon, saying people were looking in. The walls were thin enough that she could hear the neighbours talking, their laughter carrying through. Sometimes she envied the sound of it.

That was Brighton, the start of the illusion he built around her, the place where the lies began to settle in like the dampness that surrounded them.

She slipped back into memories of their first few months together and at first, he was attentive. He bought her small things like cheap trinkets and clothes, made her meals, told her she was special.

He felt safe. She was young, looking for something steady and their relationship was giving her what she needed at that point. But then it changed – as it always does.

He started picking at her: how she dressed, how she spoke, who she saw.

He chipped away at her little by little, day by day.

It didn't happen overnight, it crept in piece by piece until she stopped recognising herself. He stopped her seeing her friends, so she forced herself to stay home because the arguments weren't worth it. That's what she told herself anyway. By the time she realised how bad her relationship really was and how miserable he was making her feel, she was pregnant.

Their son Daniel was born in Brighton in March 1987.

He'd previously told her he was going into hospital for an operation that would leave him unable to have children. She thought she was doing something good for him, giving him a child before it was too late. That was another lie.

At this point I sensed a wariness about her and my instinct

told me she didn't want to bring her son into it. Regardless of who his father was, she was a mother who loved her son unconditionally and as much as she was being open with me, she still wanted to protect her child.

It was pure and simple maternal instinct – I was a mother myself, I knew the internal battle she was waging with herself at that moment.

Daniel was crucial to the story but she was reluctant to pull him in. I looked over to Alan, he'd put the camera down. He'd felt her withdrawal too. He nodded, almost imperceptibly.

I turned to her.

I told her, as carefully as I could, that people already knew who his father was, and that speaking openly might stop others filling the gaps with rumour. I was conscious even as I said it, how hard that was for a mother to hear. I held my breath. Had I said the wrong thing? Been too pushy?

She was silent for a second then she began to talk again.

After Daniel was born, the control grew worse. He didn't want her to wear make-up or colour her hair. She was only allowed to call her grandmother if he was sitting beside her listening to every word. If she took too long at the shops, he would accuse her of cheating.

She started rushing through queues and counting minutes on the walk home.

Tobin didn't stay in Brighton long after losing his job. The work dried up, the rent fell behind, and he told her they needed a fresh start.

He said Scotland would be better for all of them, cheaper and

CATHY

safer, somewhere he could get steady work. She didn't have a say and of course by then she'd stopped arguing.

They packed what little they had into his car and drove north. The journey felt endless, service stations, laybys, long silences broken by his bursts of charm. He told her they'd live near his family, that it would be good for Daniel.

She wanted to believe living in Bathgate might mean stability, but the pit in her stomach told her otherwise.

This was an explosive revelation from Cathy. At this point I had no idea how important Bathgate would become in the Peter Tobin story but I remember saying to Alan afterwards that when we got back to Scotland I needed to check the records for anything significant in Bathgate around the time he was there.

Bathgate was grey and tight-knit, the kind of place where everyone seemed to know each other's business. The house was small, on a quiet street. From the outside it looked ordinary – net curtains, a patch of grass out front – but inside it felt like the walls were closing in. He didn't know many people there, and that suited him. There was no one for her to talk to and he told neighbours he was a tradesman doing up the place.

To Cathy he said it was theirs, a proper home this time. She wanted to believe him, but everything about the house felt borrowed – the furniture, the tools, even the key in her hand.

When I asked if he ever hit her, she said not at first. He got into her head instead, made her feel stupid. Small. Later, he pushed her against a wall and held her there by the throat before letting go. He was careful not to leave marks. She said he'd throw things when he was angry – plates, cutlery, whatever was near.

Once, he threw a screwdriver at her when she was pregnant. It missed. She said it like she was talking about someone else.

He could turn kind again after the outbursts, and that confused her. He'd act loving, almost gentle and it made her think maybe things would settle.

Then he'd start again.

Once, before they moved north, he'd even checked himself into hospital and told staff his wife didn't care about him. She said it was the same act every time, weakness as a weapon, sympathy as bait.

In Bathgate, she said the air inside always smelled faintly of petrol from his tools and the hum of an electric heater that never stopped. It was the kind of noise that got into your head and made you silently curse.

The letter about the tenancy came a few months later. It said the lease was up because his employment had ended. She said she stood in the kitchen reading it twice, knowing it meant the whole life she thought she had was built on lies.

It was at this point she knew she needed to get away. She didn't tell him about the letter but started packing little things instead. Daniel's clothes, his nappies, small things belonging to her that he wouldn't notice were missing. She hid the bag under the bed and prayed he wouldn't find it. To fund her escape she started keeping coins from the shopping and hid them in the lining of her coat. This shocked me, it hammered home the reality of what she was living with, the fear, the control, the abuse.

I said as much. Cathy waved her hand in the air and her tone was almost flippant as she said fear had become part of her

CATHY

routine. It lived in her stomach, she added, constant and like hunger pangs. It was a physical sensation.

She would go about her business as usual when he was around, housework, looking after Daniel, being nice to Tobin – anything to keep up the pretence nothing was wrong.

It was normal for him to go through her purse every night but apart from the coins hidden in her coat, she also tried to squirrel away whatever money she could. A pound here, a ten pence piece there. It wasn't much but eventually she had enough to do what she needed to do.

She planned the way people plan to stay alive. No big moves, no sudden changes. She waited for a moment when he'd be gone long enough not to come back halfway through.

She taught herself to know the sound of his car engine from the street and could tell which direction it was heading.

The night she was waiting for came without warning. He suddenly announced he was going to a car auction with a friend.

As soon as his headlights disappeared from the street, she grabbed six-month-old Daniel from his cot, wrapped him in a blanket, grabbed her escape bag and left.

It was freezing outside but she walked fast, kept her head down, her heart hammering the whole time, absolutely terrified he would come careering down the street after her.

The bus station, such as it was, was nearly empty, just a few drunks and a cleaner making an attempt to mop the floor. Handing over her bag of coins with shaking hands, she bought a ticket to Portsmouth. It would mean changing in Edinburgh and this was risky because it would be the first place he would look. Tobin was street smart – he would know she didn't have the money for a train so a bus was the obvious choice and the main station was in the capital – he'd head straight there.

When she got on the coach she sat near the back, still scared. She wasn't free yet but she was close to it. Daniel slept across her lap, his small body heavy against her during the long journey. Every time the bus slowed she thought it was him. She said she didn't close her eyes once, just kept watching the road, waiting for headlights that never came.

When she reached Portsmouth the next morning, her grandparents were waiting.

She spent the day in their house, not really saying anything as they played with Daniel, made tea, and sorted him for bedtime. They gave her space to sort out her thoughts. She knew she was safe. She didn't plan her whole life out, she was just relieved to be away from him.

Then the phone rang at 2am.

It was him. He said he'd taken an overdose and was dying. He wanted her to come back to him. She hung up the phone and called the hospital he said he was in. She spoke to a nurse who said he'd live. Cathy sat in the dark until morning thinking what she could do.

"If I'd gone back," she said, "I'd never have got away again."

That phone call was the start of a pattern. He would fake illness whenever he lost control, it was a way of pulling people back in, making them feel guilty, keeping the attention on him.

Cathy had seen it before, but that night in Portsmouth showed me something I didn't yet understand. It was a pattern I would come to recognise again and again.

When he said he was dying, he was really testing whether she still cared enough to come. It wasn't the last time he would use his body as a weapon. He played sick whenever the walls started to close in on him. Illness was his excuse, his escape route, his way of twisting the story back in his favour. When he said he was unwell, people softened, they stopped asking questions, they forgot what he'd done and started to feel sorry for him. He knew exactly how to use that. He faked weakness to buy time, to shift the attention, to keep control. It was never about being sick, it was about staying one step ahead.

It was a kind of emotional blackmail, and it worked for years because people mistook it for vulnerability.

As she spoke, I thought about the types of men I'd covered over the years, the ones who knew how to twist sympathy into power. Tobin wasn't clever in any real sense, but he understood manipulation, he made people feel sorry for him. He would claim illness whenever he felt control slipping. It was a way of pulling people back in, shifting sympathy, and avoiding consequences. Weakness was part of the act. It was a trick he would play his whole life.

Cathy's grandparents gave her their spare room and helped her to care for Daniel. She said they were kind people and being with them made her feel safe for the first time in years.

During the first months after leaving him she heard nothing from Tobin so she began to believe she had left him behind. She got work again and tried to keep life as normal as possible for her son, never wanting to rely on anyone.

Then the calls began. He would ring at strange hours, usually late at night. Sometimes he said he was ill, sometimes that he needed to talk about Daniel.

Cathy said that after that call about the overdose she changed how she lived. She kept the curtains drawn and made sure Daniel was never out of sight.

She didn't report Tobin because she didn't want to draw attention to herself, and didn't want him to know she was scared. She decided the best protection was to disappear into ordinary life and hope Tobin would get fed up of chasing her.

CHAPTER TEN

DANIEL

IT WAS THE longest night of Cathy's life. By morning she hadn't slept. Then, the phone rang and it was Tobin, calm as ever, to say she'd never see Daniel again.

Long gone were the days of hiding from her violent ex-partner. He'd tracked down the mother and son and also moved to the south coast.

This was around 1992. She was still living in Portsmouth, trying to build a life that didn't involve him.

Daniel was a toddler then, all smiles and wide eyes, a happy little boy who looked like her side of the family. He was the centre of her world.

Tobin would call now and then, using that same pleasant voice that had once fooled her. He could sound gentle when he wanted to, almost reasonable. He said he only wanted to see his son. No arguments, no trouble, just a few hours together. She believed him, or wanted to. She said she thought, for once, it might be safe.

He came to collect Daniel one afternoon. He smiled, thanked her, and promised to have him home by tea time. She remembered standing at the window, watching the car pull away,

Daniel waving through the glass. The hours passed, the light faded. She made his tea and kept it warm, then it became cold, then she threw it out. By nightfall, she knew he wasn't coming back.

She called the police, her voice shaking, but they told her it was a domestic matter. Husbands and wives, fathers and mothers, these things happened all the time. They said he would bring the child back once he'd calmed down.

She hung up and sat by the phone, waiting for it to ring, her stomach in knots. Every sound outside made her jump. Every car that slowed on the street made her heart stop.

That was the longest night. In the morning she phoned the police again, begged them to do something, but they said the same thing. Domestic. Nothing to be done.

Then, hours later, Tobin called. This was when he told her he was in Scotland and would never see her son again.

She said she couldn't breathe when she heard those words.

Her grandparents tried to comfort her, but there was nothing anyone could say. She just kept saying, "He's got my boy."

That was the moment she realised he really knew how to hurt her.

Not fists, not the shouting, not the jealousy, but the pure cruelty of taking away what she loved most in the world.

After that call, she knew the police weren't going to help her.

She went straight to a solicitor who listened, and didn't waste any time. Cathy's hands were shaking as she told the story.

Within hours, they had her in front of a judge at an emergency hearing. The solicitor argued Daniel was in danger, that the

DANIEL

father had taken him without consent. The judge agreed and granted a sole custody order there and then.

As they left court, she said the solicitor turned to her and said quietly, "We'll get your boy back, I promise." It was the first time she'd felt anyone believed her. Cathy said she felt relief, but it didn't last.

The order only applied in England. It would take three days before it could be enforced in Scotland. Three days where Tobin could vanish again, cross a border, disappear into his network of lies. She said she could barely think straight. He'd called her from somewhere in Scotland, taunting her, telling her she'd never see her son again and she believed him. Every instinct told her he'd already gone for good.

That afternoon she bought a plane ticket to Edinburgh. She'd never flown before. She was terrified of heights, but she said fear of flying was nothing compared to the fear of losing Daniel.

She'd phoned ahead and when she landed, Tobin was waiting at the airport, smiling, as if it were all normal.

He drove her back to the Bathgate house – the same house she had fled from months earlier. She said she played along, talked softly, told him she wanted to try again. She cooked for him, pretended they could start over.

The next morning she convinced him to drive back down to Portsmouth with her. She said she couldn't raise Daniel in Scotland, that they'd have a better chance down south. He agreed.

When they reached Portsmouth, she told him she was going out to buy milk. Instead, she phoned the solicitor and within minutes, the bailiffs were on their way. They arrived with the custody order in hand and told Tobin to leave the house. He didn't fight and she just stood there, expressionless, watching as they escorted him out. Cathy said the door closed behind him and she could finally breathe again.

That was how she got Daniel back. No police rescue, no dramatic chase – just a mother who refused to give up. She said being with him again made her feel sick but she would do it for her son. It's what she kept telling herself during that 24 hours of sheer hell.

Despite these events, over time contact between Tobin and his son was again re-established, this time in a tightly controlled form. After years with no access, Tobin was granted limited, court-agreed overnight contact. Cathy said she did not trust him, but it was difficult for her to refuse a court arrangement. She believed the risks were contained. She was wrong.

On August 4 1993, Cathy was asleep when the phone rang at 2am and Tobin's voice came down the line, urgent sounding. He told her he was having a heart attack and needed to go to hospital.

He asked her to come and collect Daniel, who was with him on one of the court-agreed overnight visit at his flat, a short drive away from her Portsmouth home.

She didn't hesitate – she didn't care about him but she was worried what would happen to Daniel if Tobin truly was having a heart attack and he was alone with his dad. She didn't argue and got dressed quickly before heading to Leigh Park, Havant, where Tobin was now living.

DANIEL

When she got there, he was already in the building's stairwell. Daniel was with him, half asleep, carrying a small bag.

Tobin handed her the bag and said the ambulance was coming, because he had already phoned them. She noticed he was limping but when she asked him about it, he brushed it off saying he was fine and just needed to rest. She said nothing and left with Daniel.

In the morning she took Daniel to school, went to work, and tried to put it out of her mind. Then the phone rang again.

This time it was CID – they told her they needed to speak to her and that Daniel was being collected from school by officers and would be brought to her at the station. They wouldn't tell her over the phone why. When she eventually arrived at the police station, she was anxious for them to tell her what was going on.

Two teenage girls had been found in Tobin's flat, the flat where Cathy had been only hours before. Tobin had drugged and raped them but one had fought back, stabbing him in the leg, the other was badly hurt but alive.

At the subsequent trial it was said he treated them "as cruelly as a cat would a mouse".

During these terrible events, Daniel woke and went into the rooms where the girls were being held prisoner. One is even said to have asked him for help.

The teenage victims had been only feet away when Cathy collected Daniel. The bag Daniel was carrying contained a few of his father's possessions in case he never saw him again.

When Cathy and Daniel left, Tobin returned to the flat,

turned on the gas and fled. Somehow, one of the girls managed to escape and alert the police.

Sitting there listening to Cathy, I felt a jolt of disbelief at what he had done but also adrenaline at the thought of what my story would be revealing. I know that sounds harsh but I am a journalist, I wasn't there as a counsellor but as someone who would be recording this as a matter of public record. People deserved to know the truth and I knew instantly this was one of the top lines in the story – a line in a long line of revelations we would truly show what a monster this man was.

Daniel had walked in on the aftermath of one of his father's most sickening crimes.

Without knowing it, Daniel's presence may have changed what happened next.

Cathy told me the story not just to show how cruel and horrific Tobin was, but also about the wreckage he had left behind.

But she didn't understand at first, it didn't sink in and she kept thinking about Daniel going into that room, about what he might have seen. Police arranged support for Daniel in the immediate aftermath. Cathy said the impact stayed with him for years.

Tobin was gone before the police reached the flat. He left blood on the carpet, a half-empty bottle of Temazepam, and two girls barely alive. He didn't take much with him, just enough to disappear. The search began that morning and patrols spread across Hampshire and down to the coast. His car was found abandoned near the shoreline, the driver's door open, a faint smear of blood on the seat. For a few hours they

DANIEL

thought he might have gone into the sea, then they realised he was too cunning for that. He had always been good at slipping away.

He knew how to use false names, how to blend in with people who didn't ask any questions. Police traced him to hostels and shelters along the south coast where he used cash, short-term jobs, and a string of aliases. He called himself Pat McLaughlin at one address and James Kelly at another. It was the same trick he'd used for years. Crimewatch ran his photograph that week – man in his 50s with thin hair and a thin mouth.

The public were warned not to approach him. The papers called him a drifter and a conman. He was more than that, he was a predator on the move.

Cathy said she stayed inside most of the time while the police looked for him. The police phoned her everyday, believing he might come for her or try to take Daniel. Her phone had been tapped – the Home Office gave approval for this – and she was told to keep the line clear in case he called and if he did, she was not to say anything to him.

The waiting was worse than anything, the thought that he could be walking around, free, after what he did, only a few miles away.

Six weeks passed. There were sightings in Worthing, Hastings, and Brighton, each one followed by a dead end. He was always a few hours ahead. The officers handling the case said it was like chasing smoke.

Then, in early September it broke.

A man recognised him from the television. Tobin was working

casual labour in Brighton under a false name, staying in a cheap bedsit not far from the pier. When the police moved in, he didn't fight. He was skinny and still limping from the stab wound the girl had given him.

In his bag they found a change of clothes, some cash, and a knife. He told them he was planning to leave the country.

Cathy said when she heard he'd been caught she felt empty.

No joy, no relief. She told me she'd always known he'd surface in Brighton again, it was where his life had come apart, and where it seemed to circle back every time.

That arrest would lead to his first long prison sentence.

But for Cathy, it didn't close anything. That kind of fear doesn't fade, she said, you just learn to live with it.

The trial came less than a year after the attack. Winchester Crown Court was packed for the sentencing. The girls were too young to face him, but their statements were read in full. Tobin sat in the dock staring straight ahead, hands folded. When the judge called him "a danger to any woman he meets," he didn't flinch.

He pleaded guilty to rape and indecent assault. The defence said he was a man with "a troubled mind". The prosecution said he was a man who thought women were his to use.

The judge agreed. His sentence was 14 years.

Cathy followed it in the papers. She read the line about him lowering his head when the sentence was handed down and wondered if it was shame or just performance. She thought it was a performance.

In prison he kept his head down. That was his way. He didn't fight, didn't argue, never caused trouble and staff described him as polite, helpful, even mild-mannered. He worked in the chapel and the kitchens. He cleaned, he prayed, he blended in.

He started telling people he'd found God, attended every service, volunteered to polish the brass and fold the linen. To officers he was the model prisoner but to the men who lived alongside him he was something else. They said he was sly, he listened more than he spoke and he'd sit in the corner, watching, weighing people up. He told anyone who would listen that he'd been wrongly accused, that the girls had lied, that women always lied about him.

He spoke about Cathy too, as if she'd betrayed him. One prisoner said Tobin could switch moods in an instant – joking one minute, stone cold the next.

The chaplain thought he was genuine and repentant, even wrote a note in his file saying he showed signs of remorse and a desire to live a good Christian life. It went in with the others and when parole came up, that note would matter.

He spent the rest of the 1990s behind prison walls, moving between Winchester and the Isle of Wight. An unremarkable prisoner, serving tea in the chapel, quoting scripture. It was an act, but an effective one. He had learned how to disappear in plain sight.

Even so, Cathy never felt entirely free. She had security chains and peepholes fitted on her doors. The police gave her a panic alarm after he was released. She knew he had nothing left to lose and believed he might come for her.

When she spoke about those years, she didn't dramatise them, instead she spoke plainly, matter of fact. She said she had built a life in spite of it. She worked, she studied, she raised her son, but underneath it all was the certainty that he was still out there.

The first letter from him came in a white envelope, her name typed neatly in the middle but she recognised his handwriting inside straight away.

He called her "Cath" as if nothing had changed. He asked about Daniel, said he thought about him every day. Asked for photographs so he could "remember his face".

At first, the letters were full of soft words. Regret, religion, forgiveness. He said God had shown him mercy. Cathy said he wrote about God like he thought he'd invented him but it was all part of the same performance. Then the tone changed, he blamed the girls, the police, Cathy. Said they had ruined his life.

She never replied. She gave the letters to the police and asked them to monitor her phone in case he tried to call. The Home Office arranged it. For months, every ring made her jump.

One envelope held his car keys and a note telling her to do what she liked with them. She passed it straight to CID. The car turned out to be part of the case.

The letters became a pattern. Remorse, then self-pity, then blame – another kind of control.

To Cathy, it was the same man she had escaped, the same voice trying to find a way back in. She told me she could see it clearly now, the words were just another weapon.

She kept a panic alarm beside her bed.

I saw one of the letters. The handwriting was small, the words

DANIEL

packed close together. He signed it, 'Love, Peter'. It made my skin crawl.

***

Tobin walked out of prison in May 2004. Ten years served, four cut short for good behaviour.

He was almost 60 then and to the Parole Board he looked like a man finished with crime. Quiet, polite, devout. They saw an old handyman who went to the chapel and kept his head down.

The reports called him "low risk".

He'd spent years pretending to be harmless. He cleaned the chapel, washed cups in the staff kitchen, quoted the Bible.

Prison officers said he was the kind of inmate they wished they had more of. Never raised his voice. Never broke a rule.

Behind that act, the real Tobin was watching and waiting. He knew how to work a system. He knew what words to use. He told them about God, about regret. He told them he was ready to start over.

When they let him out, he headed north to Paisley. A council flat, a probation officer, a few conditions to follow. He signed on the Sex Offenders Register and promised to stay put. He never did.

He started to drift again. Different names, different towns.

"Pat McLaughlin" one week, "Peter Wilson" the next. He said he was a handyman, a decorator, a church volunteer. He turned up at parishes offering to fix broken doors and clean pews. He carried a Bible in his bag and called himself a changed man.

The system bought it. He checked in once a month, smiled

for the notes, then disappeared. Some records were lost between England and Scotland. Nobody was watching closely enough.

By 2005 he was living on the edge of the M8, in the shadow of a church that welcomed him in.

And every time I spoke to Alan about it all, he repeated a phrase we had both said many times. This was a serial killer we were dealing with.

I stayed in touch with Cathy right up to the trial. By law we couldn't print a single word of what she said until it was over, for fear of prejudicing a jury. For a journalist, that is torture. Sitting on a story you know inside out and can't use, but in a strange way, it also felt good. There's a kind of satisfaction in knowing things the world doesn't. It makes no sense really, our job is to tell, not to keep secrets, yet for a while, I was glad it was all still hush hush.

At first, staying in touch was part of the job. Follow-ups, background, keeping her side straight. But it became more than that. We talked about Daniel, about how he was coping, about what it had done to them both.

***

Early in 2007 Cathy rang to say Daniel wanted to speak to me. The trial was still ahead of us, but already Tobin was the bogeyman Scotland feared – his name was whispered by people as if saying his name aloud would bring him to their door.

Cathy told me her son had questions and that he wanted his own say. At 17, he was old enough now to decide that for himself. This was another exclusive for the paper – it would be

DANIEL

the first time the son of Peter Tobin would speak in public. It was huge for us, a massive scoop and the bosses were happy. Alan and I were flown down to Portsmouth again to meet with Daniel and Cathy.

When we met, he was polite and guarded, a young man who learned early that words could be dangerous. He had his mother's manner, calm on the surface and wary underneath. He told me he trusted me because she had.

I looked at him, thinking how strange it was to be face to face with the boy who had once been caught in Tobin's world. The same child who had been caught up in events in Leigh Park years earlier, far beyond what any child should have had to deal with. Daniel was a confident, well assured young man. I could tell he and his mother were close, he was very protective of her and she of him. Understandable really, considering everything they'd been through together. But she had raised a well grounded, polite man and I was impressed.

He wanted to talk about Leigh Park. This surprised me but straight away he told me he didn't remember much about that night, only fragments of noise, raised voices, and confusion.

He said it came back to him in flashes, the sound of shouting, the clatter of something falling, then silence. He was too young to understand what he had walked into.

He said what stayed with him most wasn't the violence itself, but what came after.

The police cars, the questions, his mother's face when they told her what had happened.

He said he used to look for his dad in crowds when he was

small, even after everything. Part of him still wanted an answer that made sense. When I asked if he hated his father, he thought for a long time before speaking.

"I don't hate him," he said. "I just don't understand him. I don't think I ever will."

He said he'd stopped using the name Tobin years before. It wasn't about shame, just survival, he didn't want people to hear it and look at him differently. He'd learned to measure who he could trust by how they reacted when they found out. He said his mother had tried to protect him from it all, but the past had a way of showing up anyway. Every time Tobin's name was in the news, the memories came back. He said it was like being dragged into something he hadn't chosen.

As he spoke, I could hear Cathy in his voice – the same self-control, the same need to keep emotion in check. He said he'd heard what she had said to me for the paper and that she had been right to tell it.

"It was her story too," he told me.

I asked what he wanted people to know about growing up as Peter Tobin's son. He said he didn't want pity, and he didn't want headlines. He just wanted people to understand that being his son didn't make him part of it.

"I've spent my whole life proving I'm not him," he said.

That was the line that stayed with me. He told me he wanted to leave the past alone, but the past had other ideas. It was a one-time interview. We ran it after Tobin's trial.

I thought Daniel was a lovely young man with a bright future ahead of him. Polite, thoughtful, the kind of person you

DANIEL

wanted to see do well after everything he had lived through. He'd carried more than most people ever should, and was still standing.

At the time, I believed the worst was behind him. That the story had finally reached its end.

Of course, it hadn't. None of us knew then what was still waiting to be uncovered.

Cathy and Daniel had survived what most people wouldn't.

That, in the end, was the story. Not him. Them.

CHAPTER ELEVEN

THE ANGELIKA KLUK TRIAL: PART ONE

WEEK ONE

I knew the High Court in Edinburgh well. I had sat through a few murder trials, watched stories unfold from the press bench and seen lives unravel in awful ways. The place never lost its chill, even on a spring morning.

The trial began on 23 March 2007. Almost six months had passed since Tobin was charged in connection with Angelika Kluk's death. In Scotland that kind of delay is not unusual, major cases move slowly because every detail has to be checked and The Crown does not take chances. Every statement, photograph and piece of evidence must stand up to scrutiny before a case reaches the jury.

A Scottish jury has 15 members. A simple majority decides the verdict. Eight people must agree for a conviction. There are three possible outcomes: guilty, not guilty and not proven. The last one is unique to Scotland, although at the time of writing, Scotland has legislated to abolish it. Not Proven carries the same result as an acquittal but it leaves a shadow of doubt behind it. Neither innocent nor guilty: it is a terrible verdict and its abolition has been fiercely campaigned for but not universally welcomed by all.

There is no hung jury in Scotland. If fewer than eight believe the accused is guilty, the case is over.

Murder trials are heard in the High Court, Scotland's top tier of criminal justice. The Crown is represented by an Advocate Depute instructed by the Lord Advocate. The defence is led by an Advocate or Solicitor Advocate. A High Court judge presides over it all. The process is formal, deliberate and steeped in tradition.

Usually I didn't go to court and in this case I wasn't in court every day – we had dedicated court reporters as it's a specialist skill covering trials and hearings although all reporters must have an up to date working knowledge of the Scottish legal system. I would only be sent to cover a trial if an agency wasn't or the paper had a story exclusively but it was a rare thing for me to be inside the courtroom.

I was a little envious of my court colleagues, I wanted to be there to see it all unfold.

However, *The Sunday Mail* was leaving the day-to-day trial reports for the dailies to print.

After all, we wouldn't be out until the weekend. I was working on other stories and keeping in touch with Cathy Wilson. We had her story and Daniel's ready to go, depending on the verdict.

The street outside the court was already crowded with journalists and camera crews. They knew the routine, claiming their spots and chatting as they waited. In Scotland, media circles are tight, we all know each other, but rivalry hums quietly under the surface.

The regulars were already there, the ones who seemed to live on the court steps, notebooks in hand, waiting for the doors to open.

Usually, they handled trials like this on their own, but not today. This one had drawn in everyone: national desks, foreign crews, even Polish television. From the live shots, it looked less like a murder trial and more like a media circus.

Inside the court, the Advocate Depute for the Crown was Dorothy Bain QC. She wasn't the type to play to the gallery. Calm, exact, and impossible to rattle. I'd watched her before in other murder trials and she never missed a detail. When she spoke, the room went quiet. She had a reputation for being one of the sharpest prosecutors in the country, the kind brought in when the Crown wanted to make sure nothing slipped through the cracks.

She took the jury through Angelika Kluk's final days, slow and steady. The Polish student who had come to Scotland for the summer. The church that had taken her in.

The man who worked there under a false name. Each fact landed where she wanted it to.

During the breaks, reporter friends called or texted from the corridor, passing on what they'd caught inside. Angelika's name echoed through their updates, and the words "the cellar" came up more than once. Everyone knew that was where she had been found[1].

Brendan decided later that day to send me to the court to get some colour for when we could tell the stories. Colour meant atmosphere, the mood of the place, the way people moved or spoke.

I watched the doors as people came out for air. Some of the younger reporters looked pale and tired. I didn't ask what they had heard, the early days of a murder trial always carried a weight. Even without the details, everyone knew what was coming.

When the court adjourned for lunch, a few of the press crossed over to where I sat with Alan Simpson having a coffee. They asked about Cathy. I told them she wasn't giving interviews and they backed off, some of them knew me well enough not to push it. Others tried their luck anyway.

That afternoon, Bain went deeper into the evidence. The Crown's case was that Tobin had attacked Angelika in St Patrick's Church, then hid her body in a cramped space used for storage and repairs. Her body, the crown said, was found beneath the floorboards of the sacristy, hidden under a hatch and covered with sheets of wood. Tobin had taken time to cover the area neatly, moving boxes and tools back into place before carrying on as if nothing had happened. He ate with the priests, helped with chores, even joined them for evening prayers while her body lay just feet below.

---

1   This is how journalists and people would describe where Angelika's body was found. In court it was later revealed she was actually discovered under the sacristy in a space accessed by a trapdoor

Bain explained that police had searched the church for several days before the discovery. They had followed every corridor, checked every locked room, and drained outside drains and ducts. In the end, it was the smell that led them to her body.

One of the officers noticed a new section of wood and a change in the air. When they lifted the hatch, they found her. It was the kind of detail that stuck in your head. Hearing it second-hand was bad enough, I could only imagine what it was like to sit in the courtroom while she spoke. By the time the first day ended, the light had started to fade over Edinburgh. Reporters were phoning in their copy before deadlines. The television crews broke down their kit and loaded it into vans. Coffee cups and cables were left scattered across the pavement outside the High Court. It was quiet again, the way it always was after a big news day, with only the sound of engines starting and footsteps fading into the distance.

I spoke to Cathy on the phone.

"It's started then," she said in a flat tone.

I nodded and answered, "It has."

Neither of us said much else, there wasn't much else to say.

The first full week of the trial opened with the church and the people who had lived and worked around it. The jury were told how Angelika Kluk had made her home at St Patrick's, and how Peter Tobin had turned up there under the name Pat McLaughlin. From the press room and the corridor, we pieced it together from what reporters inside sent out during breaks.

The early witnesses were parish volunteers. They spoke about Angelika cleaning, polishing, and helping wherever she could. Tobin had arrived through the Loaves and Fishes charity, offering to paint and repair things around the church. People said he seemed quiet, polite, and eager to please.

Midweek, police evidence began. From what filtered out, the search of the church was described in detail. Officers looked through every room, every cupboard, before finding the section of floor that looked freshly boarded and when they lifted it, they found her body beneath the hatch in the sacristy.

The following day, detectives took the jury through the days after Angelika vanished. They said Tobin left Glasgow the next morning, travelling south under a false name. He was traced to a hospital in Kent, where he had been admitted after taking an overdose.

By the end of the week, the picture was clear enough for those of us outside to follow it. The Crown's case was that Angelika trusted him, and that he killed her and tried to hide what he had done. The Crown still had forensics to present, but already there was no doubt who they believed was responsible. Outside the High Court, cameras waited in the cold, reporters phoned in their lines and the air around the court felt heavy with the story's weight. Everyone knew the hard evidence was still to come.

WEEK TWO

At the start of the second week, while the trial carried on, Brendan called and told me I was going to Poland. He wanted more background on Angelika, who she had been before Scotland. Before the headlines. It felt like an odd call to make in the middle of a murder trial, but that was how it worked, if there was a story worth chasing, you went.

Alan Simpson came with me. We flew to Gdańsk a few days later. It was early April and unseasonably warm. Poland was beautiful in the spring and not for the first time I wondered what made Angelika swap it for Scotland.

For the first time in months, I didn't need a coat and the air smelled faintly of salt from the Baltic.

I should have felt excited, but I was anxious.

The trial was still moving at full pace back home and every morning I worried it might end without me. I kept checking the time difference, imagining the courtroom, wondering what evidence was being shown that day. I felt like I had stepped out of the centre of the story and it was strange to be watching from the sidelines.

We stayed for four or five days, tracing her life before Glasgow. Gdańsk was calm, cobbled and bright. We carried a photograph of Angelika, the one used in the papers, and showed it around the university until someone recognised her.

That was how we found her closest friend, Agnieszka Bastian. She had studied Scandinavian languages with Angelika at Gdańsk University. We met in a small café near the old town. The sun caught the steam rising from our coffee cups. Agnieszka was 24, thoughtful and softly spoken.

She told me Angelika had been quiet and serious.

"She was really hardworking," she said. "By far the best student. She wanted to study all the time, and if she wasn't doing that, she was at church."

THE ANGELIKA KLUK TRIAL: PART ONE

Agnieszka said Angelika never went to parties and barely spoke to any of the boys on their course.

"When you got her on her own she was sweet. She would giggle at my stories and blush if I mentioned boyfriends. But she never dated anyone. That just wasn't her."

She remembered the last time they saw each other. Angelika mentioned she was going back to Scotland for the summer.

"I asked if she liked it there," Agnieszka said. "She said she loved it and was going to stay in the same place as before. A church."

When the reports came out during the trial about Angelika's relationships in Glasgow, Agnieszka shook her head.

"The Angelika we are hearing about isn't the girl we knew. It's hard to connect those two people."

Later that day I spoke to her tutor, Dr Hieronim Chojnacki. He said she had been well liked and incredibly intelligent.

"An intensely religious person but also very private," he told me. "We all miss her a great deal."

I should have felt proud to be there, but I was uneasy the whole time, every update from home made me restless. I kept thinking I should be closer, I had spent years fighting to be at the centre of big stories and now I was thousands of miles away.

The only bright spots were the people who spoke about her as she really was, and the strange comfort of being in Poland itself. It was the first time I had been in my grandfather's homeland. Standing in the old town square, hearing the language he once spoke, I felt something shift. It steadied me and for a few moments, the case and its noise faded.

When we flew home, the trial was still underway but the rhythm of it had changed: moving on to the forensics and witness statements, the grim details of the body discovery. I went straight from the airport to the newsroom. The story had never really stopped but the first days of shock gave way to focus. The same faces turned up early, clutching coffees and notebooks. Edinburgh had that half-awake look it gets in spring, when the light is starting to brighten again and you can just smell better weather is coming.

Inside the court, the benches were full again. The Crown called more witnesses, this time to explain what the science could prove. Professor Anthony Busuttil described Angelika's injuries in detail. The wounds were extensive, he said, to the head, the chest and the face. She had been alive for part of the attack and the marks showed she tried to fight back. The words were clinical but the meaning was brutal.

Each picture made it harder to separate the story from the reality of what had been done to her. Reporters, used to hearing such graphic details, stopped writing. Even the ushers seemed to move more quietly.

Phone records showed that Angelika's mobile was used after her death. Calls were made and messages sent. The prosecution said Tobin had done that to make people believe she was still alive. It was deliberate, they said, a trick to buy time.

Later that week, the focus shifted back to St Patrick's. Among the parish witnesses due to appear was Father Nugent, the priest who had taken Tobin in. His name came up often that week, though his evidence was still to come.

Parish witnesses spoke again about the days leading up to Angelika's disappearance. Some had seen her cleaning in the church on the Sunday she went missing, others said she had looked tired but cheerful, ready to go home to Poland.

Outside, the press huddled under umbrellas between sessions. The weather had turned again, a fine rain settling on the cobbles. Reporters traded lines quietly. Screams. DNA. False names. It was the week the story became something darker, heavier.

I kept in touch with Cathy as the trial went on. She didn't want to hear the details but she wanted to know how long it would last. I told her the truth, it was only the second week and there was still more to come.

WEEK THREE

The third week opened cold and quiet and reporters gathered under the stone arches, shaking rain from their coats and sharing cigarettes. Nobody said much. Inside, the benches were full again and The Crown picked up where they left off, calling witnesses whose words carried more weight than photographs. Professor Anthony Busuttil was recalled briefly to clarify details that no one in the room would ever forget. Angelika's body showed signs of restraint. The strikes had been sustained and violent and she had been alive when the attack began.

The air in the courtroom was still as he spoke, even the court officers moved carefully. The jurors looked pale, everyone knew they were hearing the worst of it now. Later that week, Cathy

Wilson gave her evidence and the moment her name was called, Tobin lifted his head. It was the first time anyone had seen him move, his eyes followed her as she walked to the witness box, tracking every step.

She didn't look at him. She kept her eyes on the judge and spoke quietly, answering each question with care. She told the jury how she had met him as a teenager in Brighton. He had seemed kind and charming at first, the sort of man who could make anyone feel safe, but once they married, everything changed. He controlled what she wore, where she went, who she spoke to. He kept her close and made sure she stayed that way.

She said he could change in a second, one moment calm, the next violent. She told the court he would threaten her, that he had once held a knife to her and said he would bury her under the floorboards if she ever left him. The words hung in the air. Nobody moved.

When she finally did leave him, she thought she was free, but not long after, he took their son Daniel and disappeared.

Cathy told the jury she had spent years afraid of him, she had built a new life and stayed away. Her voice remained steady, even when the questions touched on things most people could never say out loud. She didn't look at him once, not even when she left the stand. He watched her all the way out. It was the only time during the entire trial that Tobin lifted his head.

After that came the civilian witnesses. Leigh Brown, a woman from a nearby flat, took the stand. She was small, neatly dressed and visibly nervous as she told the court she was watching television on the afternoon of 24 September 2006 when she heard a scream. She said it was sharp and sudden, the kind that makes your heart stop. She went to her window but saw nothing. The sound had already died.

Her husband, Andrew Brown, confirmed it. He heard it too from the kitchen. The scream lasted only a moment, but they both remembered it clearly and the silence that followed was worse.

That single scream became one of the most haunting moments of the trial.

Later that day, Father Nugent took the stand for the first time.

During the police investigation, Father Nugent had been treated as another witness. He opened the door to officers, made them tea, and told them what he could. He said Angelika had helped around the church, that she stayed in a spare room, that she was like a daughter to him. The detectives took notes, thanked him, and moved on.

But as the investigation continued, parts of his story began to shift. Other witnesses said Angelika often stayed in his quarters, not just in the parish rooms. A few mentioned seeing them together late at night, talking quietly in the presbytery kitchen. When detectives compared statements, the timeline did not fit. They went back to him and he hesitated more this time, less sure of what to say. When they asked again about Angelika, his tone changed. He said there had been a lapse, a moment of weakness. He called it "a sin of lustfulness".

The information stayed confidential through the investigation. Only the police and Crown lawyers knew what he had said. It did not become public until the trial, when he took the stand and repeated it under oath.

It was likely agreed with prosecutors that the Crown should raise it first, in case the defence had planned to use it to undermine him. That was standard practice, a way of controlling how the truth came out. Nugent's appearance drew a murmur across the room. He looked older, thinner, and his voice was quieter than it had been in the interviews he gave in the days after Angelika vanished.

He admitted that he had once been intimate with her. It happened the previous year, he said. A lapse, a weakness, something he had regretted deeply. Advocate Depute Dorothy Bain QC asked if Angelika had lived with him during her visits to Glasgow. He said she had, and that he treated her like a daughter until the brief affair blurred the boundaries. He said they both tried to move on, to keep working together for the good of the parish and he denied ever suspecting Tobin was dangerous.

Nugent described Tobin, known to him as "Pat McLaughlin", as polite and eager to help. He said he believed him to be a good worker who had fallen on hard times and he told the court he gave him food and a bed because that was what the Church was supposed to do. His voice cracked slightly when Bain asked if he had known Tobin was a convicted sex offender.

"No," he said. "I didn't."

Bain asked whether Angelika ever spokn of being frightened. Nugent hesitated before replying that she had not, he said he believed she was safe under the roof of the church. It was a heartbreaking statement and you could feel the unease ripple through the room. When I saw this evidence come through the wires, I knew the trade well enough to guess what the next day's papers would lead with. Not Angelika herself, and not the full weight of what had been done to her, but the priest, the church, the scandal of what had taken place. A man in a position of authority in a religious setting where a young woman should have been safe. I knew how the story would be framed and, not for the first time, it made me feel ashamed. Not because the facts shouldn't be reported, but because I knew how easily the balance would tilt, how quickly Angelika would be reduced to a supporting character in a story that traded on shock rather than responsibility. I wasn't personally responsible for how those stories would be written, but that knowledge still makes me cringe.

After Nugent stepped down, the parish witnesses returned. Agnes Szynkowska spoke about Angelika's unease. She said her friend once mentioned that Tobin watched her too closely when she was cleaning. Angelika had laughed about it at the time but admitted she did not like being alone with him. Another parishioner, Margaret O'Donnell, told the jury Tobin had been "overly familiar".

He called the young women "darlin" and "sweetheart". She said it made her uncomfortable, but back then it was easy to brush off, nobody imagined what he was capable of. By the end of the week, the picture was clear. A man posing as a handyman had lived among them, earning their trust, attending Mass, praying beside them and hiding a monster's secret behind the language of faith. Outside the court, reporters stood quietly as they phoned through their updates. Everyone was talking about Nugent, they were all feeling the weight of it. That night, I called Cathy as she was in Edinburgh. She didn't ask for details, she didn't want to hear what had been said, she only wanted to know if it was nearly over. I told her the truth, it wasn't. The trial was still climbing towards its worst parts, and there was more yet to come.

CHAPTER TWELVE

THE ANGELIKA KLUK TRIAL: PART TWO

WEEK FOUR

By the fourth week, the trial was part of Edinburgh's routine. The same faces turned up each morning, the same police officers took their seats, and the same hush fell when the judge entered. The shock of the early days had gone and what was left felt colder. Detective Constable Paul McHugh of Strathclyde Police described searching Tobin's room and finding Angelika's belongings hidden behind a toolbox: her handbag and keys. He said it looked deliberate, not forgotten. The court fell silent as he read out each item.

The evidence had started to close around him and by the end of the week, the prosecution's case was set. Every small detail linked to another, the soil, the fibres, the DNA, the belongings, the movements. Together they built a picture of one man trying to erase what he had done. That Friday the Crown rested. Advocate Depute Bain thanked the witnesses and closed her folder. The room stayed quiet. Everyone knew what that silence meant. In the hall, reporters said the same thing in different ways. It was over for him, you could feel it. That evening I copied my notes out by hand, the way I always did when a story mattered. I didn't realise it then, but this was the turning point. Everything from here would lead to the verdict that changed everything.

WEEK FIVE

The following Monday the defence began. It felt like a different trial. The room was the same but the mood was not. The tension that had hung over the benches for weeks changed into something colder, more deliberate. Donald Findlay QC stood to address the court. He was one of Scotland's best-known defence advocates, a man with presence, wit and confidence. His voice carried easily across the room. He began by telling the jury that the Crown's case relied on assumption, that there were gaps in the timeline, and suspicion was not proof.

He reminded them Tobin's DNA could have been found in the church for innocent reasons. He worked there, cleaned, repaired, and touched things. It was wrong, he said, to assume guilt from contact alone. He questioned the reliability of the witnesses, especially those from the parish. He suggested that after the murder they might have reinterpreted harmless behaviour as sinister. He spoke for almost two hours without notes. His arguments were polished, but the mood in the court did not shift. The evidence left little room for doubt. The defence called only one witness, a tradesman who had done repair work at St Patrick's. He said he had seen Tobin and Angelika speaking together and that nothing seemed unusual. The Crown did not challenge him for long. The jurors took notes, polite but unmoved. Findlay then read from Tobin's police interviews. Tobin claimed he left Glasgow before Angelika disappeared, that he had travelled south for work and someone else must have been responsible. The words sounded hollow. The jury had already seen the phone records, they knew he was lying.

Tobin sat motionless in the dock as the defence spoke for him. He looked older than his years and his hair was thin, his skin pale under the courtroom lights. He rarely lifted his eyes. Sometimes he scribbled notes on a pad, sometimes he simply stared at the floor. He gave nothing away. The week dragged on and outside, the weather shifted between rain and a weak sun. The same reporters gathered on the steps every morning, their chat much quieter now. The sense of inevitability had set in. By Thursday, the defence was running out of ground. Findlay's tone had softened, he spoke less about evidence and more about doubt. He said Tobin's past did not define him and warned the jury not to be swayed by emotion. But there was little left to argue.

Cathy had come up to Edinburgh that week. She stayed away from the court while the defence spoke but wanted to be there for the end. I kept in touch with her every night, either by phone or meeting her for coffee away from the press pack. She was calm but restless. She said she wanted to see it through. By Friday afternoon, the defence had finished. The judge told the jury they would hear closing speeches the following week. The reporters began packing up, already knowing how this story would end. That evening, I walked with Cathy down the Royal Mile. The streetlights reflected on the wet cobbles.

She spoke quietly.

"It doesn't feel like it's really happening."

I told her it never does until it's over.

WEEK SIX

By the start of the sixth week, the trial had become a siege. The same reporters lined the steps each morning and the television vans idled on the High Street. The jury had sat through weeks of evidence, photographs, exhibits and testimony. Everything now hinged on the final arguments.

The atmosphere inside the court that morning felt heavy. Even the sound of chairs scraping the floor made people turn and the clerks spoke in whispers. The jury filed in slowly, some with dark circles under their eyes. They had been living with Angelika's name for six weeks, listening to every detail of her last hours. The weight of that was written on their faces.

Dorothy Bain rose first for the Crown, her tone calm and deliberate. She reminded the jury of the evidence. The DNA. The blood. She spoke about the brutality of the attack, about how Angelika fought for her life, and how the man who killed her, hid her body and carried on as if nothing had happened.

She told them Tobin took refuge in the church, not because of faith but because it gave him cover. He played the part of a handyman and a worshipper while planning violence. She said he used religion as a disguise, deceiving good people who trusted him.

Her closing words were quiet but sharp.

"He thought he could hide behind God," she said. "But the truth found him in the end."

When she sat down, the court was silent. You could hear paper rustling, the faint creak of the dock as Tobin shifted in his seat. Nobody moved for several seconds. It takes a lot to quiet a courtroom full of press and lawyers, but she had managed it.

Donald Findlay stood next, reminding the jury that doubt was not weakness but justice. He said the case against Tobin was powerful but not perfect and urged them to remember there were no witnesses to the killing, no confession, and that circumstantial evidence, no matter how strong, still required proof beyond reasonable doubt.

His delivery was precise and theatrical, but even he seemed to sense the outcome. The jury listened without expression. The photographs and forensics had already spoken louder than any argument.

Reporters scribbled fragments of Findlay's speech, the kind of phrases that would make headlines later. "Coincidence", "assumption", "reasonable doubt". He used them like weapons, each one thrown gently into the air to see if it would land. He was good at that. He knew how to fill a room with questions but the jurors barely looked up from their notes. They had already seen too much.

The next morning, the judge gave his directions and reminded the jury of their duty, that the verdict must be based only on evidence, not emotion. He explained the options open to them: guilty, not guilty, or not proven, then he sent them out to deliberate.

By the time the jury retired, the shape of the violence was no longer in doubt. What remained unsaid in the courtroom would later be named by the judge. The jury filed out one by one, their faces blank. The heavy wooden doors closed behind them and the sound echoed through the hall. Outside, the corridors filled with noise again. Reporters started making calls. The buzz of the vending machine, the squeak of shoes on the polished floor, all of it felt sharper after hours of silence.

Alan Simpson was outside. He was among the photographers, all given the same instruction: Get a picture of Tobin being led into the prison wagon.

"Not managed to get a picture yet. They keep hiding him. Why would you protect that monster?" Alan said quietly.

He was right. When he left the dock, even in handcuffs, Tobin walked as if he was heading to the shops, not back to a cell that would end his life in daylight.

Reporters gathered outside, smoking and pacing the street. The hours passed slowly and by late afternoon, word spread that the jury had returned. The cameras were ready before anyone spoke.

Cathy had come to the court that morning. She was waiting for this moment. I stayed with her that day. It was my job to make sure no one else got to her before we ran our story, but it was more than that, by then I cared about her. She had lived through hell, and this was the day she would finally find some form of closure.

We stood together as the doors opened and people began filing back into the building. She didn't move and her hands stayed clasped tightly in front of her.

We didn't go in, neither of us could face it. Instead, we walked round the corner to a small café and sat down. From there we couldn't see the court or hear the crowd, it was just the two of us, waiting. The noise, the cameras, the verdict – all of it felt far away.

I'd seen a lot of people face the men who'd destroyed their lives, but never anyone so steady. Cathy didn't cry, didn't tremble, didn't even blink. She had decided long ago that he would never see her break again. She wasn't there for him, she was there to see the system do what it had failed to do before.

Inside, the clerk read the verdict aloud. Guilty.

Tobin did not move. He looked straight ahead as the judge told him he would spend the rest of his life in prison. The minimum term was set at 21 years. He nodded once, as if the number meant nothing.

I wasn't in the courtroom when the verdict came, but I knew how he'd look. I'd seen it before. No guilt, no relief, no anger. Just calm. Not courage. Not defiance. Emptiness. Whatever part of him had once been human was gone a long time ago.

When it was over, people began to breathe again. Reporters ran for phones, families cried quietly in the gallery. The Crown gathered their papers and left.

Reporters moved like a tide, pushing through to the doors, the sound of their voices filled the corridor again.

"Life. Minimum 21."

Outside, Tobin's calm finally cracked.

As he was led from the court, he kicked out at photographers. He made contact – *Scottish Sun* photographer Peter Kelly was crouched low for a picture and Tobin's foot caught him. For a moment Tobin's mask slipped. The man who had sat so still through weeks of evidence showed what was underneath. Rage. Sudden and ugly. Then he was gone, taken away under guard.

Cathy and I spoke for a while inside the café, then it was time to leave. I walked her to the car. When we reached it, she turned to me.

"I keep wondering what would've happened if I hadn't left."

I didn't have an answer, there isn't one. I told her what reporters always tell survivors, that she did the right thing, that she saved herself and her son. But it sounded hollow even as I said it.

"I'm glad it's done," she said. Then, after a pause, "I just keep thinking about that poor girl. But it's over now."

She was pleased he was found guilty, but she wasn't celebrating. She said it didn't feel like a victory, more like the end of something that had been haunting her for years. But it was done.

And for the first time in years, for her, it really was.

I sat in the dark for a long time that night. The TV in the corner was showing the evening news. Tobin's face filled the screen again, the same photo I had seen a hundred times. It didn't look like victory. It looked like unfinished business.

Outside the High Court the media were still packing up. Cameras folded, satellite vans pulling away from the kerb, the sound of engines echoing against the wet stone. It was a typical Edinburgh evening, damp and heavy with the smell of rain.

I watched for a while, half relieved it was over, half dreading what might come next. By then I had already written most of my piece and it was running that weekend, the only story in town. Everyone in the Scottish press knew I had Cathy and Daniel's story sewn up, and that our exclusive would lead the paper. It should have felt like triumph, but it didn't. I had broken plenty of front pages before, but this one felt important. This story wasn't about the chase or the byline, it was about what he had done, and what it had taken from so many people.

Looking back, even then I felt certain he was a serial killer. Call it instinct, experience, or just the feeling that comes from years of watching the same pattern appear again and again. That certainty only grew when I began reading the stories of his other wives and the women who had escaped him. Every one of them described the same pattern: the charm, the control, the violence, the sudden disappearances. It was all there, hiding in plain sight.

That weekend should have felt like an ending, but it didn't. The paper hit the stands on Sunday morning and my phone didn't stop ringing. Editors, producers, other reporters, everyone wanted more. I sat at my kitchen table with the paper in front of me and felt no pride, only a cold certainty that this was not the end of Peter Tobin's story. The trial had closed one chapter, but it didn't feel finished. I still had questions, and I wasn't the only one.

CHAPTER THIRTEEN

THE DAMAGE DONE

THE TRIAL MIGHT have been over, but the story wasn't. The day after the verdict, the High Court felt different. The crowds were gone, the cameras packed away, yet the place still held a kind of charge.

Inside, Tobin was back in the dock for sentencing but not before he pulled off one last trick. He leaned forward, head bowed, one hand pressed to his chest. A nurse and a guard stood close beside him. He muttered that he felt faint, that he couldn't breathe. The judge ordered a short break while the medic checked him over. It was theatre and everyone in the room knew it. He had sat through six weeks of evidence without a word, and now that he faced life in prison, he wanted the attention back on him.

When the hearing resumed, the court was silent. Only the judge spoke. In sentencing, the judge described the murder as following a rape.

From the sentencing remarks of Lord Menzies, High Court of Justiciary, Edinburgh, 4 May 2007:

"In the course of my time in the law I have seen many bad

men, and I have heard evidence about many terrible crimes which have been committed, but I have heard no case more tragic nor more terrible than this one.

"The Advocate Depute described what you did to Angelika Kluk as an atrocity, and that word aptly describes what you did to this young woman.

"Any case of rape is serious; any case of murder is serious, but what you did to Angelika Kluk was inhuman.

"To bind her hands, gag her so tightly that her face was misshapen when her body was found, to rape her, beat her about the head repeatedly with a table leg fracturing her skull, stab her repeatedly about her chest and body, and then drag her through the church and dump her body under the floorboards as so much rubbish, all this shows utter contempt and disdain for the life of an innocent young woman with her whole life ahead of her.

"You are an evil man.

"Under our law, there is only one sentence which I can impose in respect of charge two, namely life imprisonment, and I sentence you to life imprisonment.

"In addition, the law requires me to specify what is called 'the punishment part' of that sentence...

"Having regard to the awful circumstances of this crime, together with the two other offences on this indictment of which you have been convicted, and also to your record of previous convictions which includes serious sexual offences, I impose a punishment part of 21 years.

"In addition, it is clear from your record of previous convictions that you are a danger to women and a serial sex offender.

"I place you on the Sex Offenders Register indefinitely."

Lord Menzies' voice was stern but level.

Tobin didn't flinch. He didn't move. He kept his head down, hands clasped in front of him, as if the words meant nothing.

He just stared at the floor. It was over.

Cathy followed it from a distance, she didn't want to see him again, not even for that. When the news came through, she called me and said quietly, "Good. That's it then."

The days that followed were chaos.

The Church was in crisis and the press could smell it. The revelations about Father Nugent had broken during the trial, but the full weight of them hit afterwards. He had admitted in the witness box to a "sin of lustfulness" with Angelika. It wasn't gossip anymore, it was fact, spoken under oath in front of a jury and the world.

The Archdiocese of Glasgow suspended him almost immediately. They said it was temporary while they reviewed his conduct, but everyone knew what that meant. His parishioners were furious and heartbroken in equal measure. Some defended him, saying he had been used by Tobin like everyone else, others said he had betrayed the Church and the girl he had promised to protect.

The story dominated headlines for weeks. It wasn't only about Tobin anymore, it was about trust, faith, and hypocrisy. The image of St Patrick's Church, once a place of refuge, was now a crime scene in the public mind. The photographs of the red sandstone building were everywhere, always with the same caption underneath: The church where Angelika Kluk was murdered.

I went back there after the trial. The police tape was gone, but the air still felt sad and people passed quickly, eyes down, as if the place carried bad luck. Inside, candles were lit but few stayed to pray and the pews that had once been full were mostly empty. You could feel it, the beginning of the end for the once historic chapel.

In 2023 the Catholic Church announced that St Patrick's would be closing its doors for good, bringing an end to more than a century of worship.

The Archdiocese tried to contain the damage. Statements were issued, apologies made, committees formed. It didn't matter, the story was too big. The public had seen a priest admit an affair with a parish worker who had died under his roof, murdered by a man he had welcomed in. It was the kind of scandal the Church couldn't explain away.

Nugent disappeared from sight and for months there were sightings, rumours that he was drinking heavily, that he had been moved between parishes, that he was being protected. The truth was he was broken. He had lost his parish, his calling, and his faith in himself. I didn't see him again until much later, but when I did, he looked like a man who had been hollowed out.

In the weeks after the verdict, something uglier began to surface and the headlines started to shift. It wasn't enough that Tobin had been convicted, now the spotlight turned on Angelika herself.

Some papers ran stories hinting she had been reckless, that she had blurred boundaries, that her relationship with Father Nugent somehow explained what had happened to her. It was cruel and it was wrong. She was a young woman far from home, working in a church she believed was safe. But once a story like that starts, it takes on a life of its own.

There were whispers about her private life, about who she had trusted and why. Some of the same newspapers which wrote about her kindness and faith while she was missing were now pulling her apart. It happens more often than people think. The victim becomes a character in someone else's narrative and they stop being real.

For me, that was one of the hardest parts to watch. Angelika's life was reduced to headlines and innuendo. She was spoken about as if she had brought trouble on herself, as if her choices led her to Tobin. She was the victim of a predator, not the architect of her own death.

Cathy read some of those stories too. She told me she couldn't believe how quickly people turned on the dead, that Angelika deserved better. I agreed. It felt like she had been failed twice, first by the man who killed her, and then by a media machine that couldn't resist scandal over truth.

Father Nugent's life never recovered after the trial. He was suspended, stripped of his parish, and quietly moved out of St Patrick's. The Church called it "pastoral leave" but everyone knew he was being hidden. He drank more, stopped answering calls, and withdrew from those who had once defended him.

In November 2008 he was charged with contempt of court for refusing to hand over his diaries to police. He said they were private, that they contained confessions from parishioners. The judge disagreed, he was found guilty and given a suspended sentence. By then he was living alone in a small flat in Glasgow's West End. His health was failing and his reputation was in ruins.

He died on 19 January 2009, aged 66. His body was found in that flat after neighbours raised the alarm. There was no sign of foul play. The Procurator Fiscal (who has oversight on all sudden/unnatural deaths in Scotland) said it was natural causes, heart failure brought on by years of drinking.

When I heard, I wasn't surprised. He had been on a slow path to that ending since the day Angelika's body was found. The Church released a short statement calling him a man who had "served his parish faithfully". They didn't mention the scandal, the affair, or the trial. They never do.

I didn't feel anger when I read it, just sadness. He wasn't a villain, not in the way Tobin was, he was a weak man who made a terrible mistake and spent the rest of his life paying for it. His name will always be tied to Angelika's, and that is its own punishment.

The news of Father Nugent's death brought the story flooding back.

Tobin was already serving his life sentence, but his name was never far from the headlines. When Nugent's body was found, every newsroom in Scotland ran the same line: Priest linked to Angelika Kluk murder found dead in Glasgow flat.

The phone calls started early that morning. I was a freelance reporter having left *The Scottish Sun* to go at it alone.

Editors wanted fresh quotes, old contacts, background files. Reporters were sent to his block of flats before the ambulance had even left. It was like the trial all over again, the same faces, the same rush for copy, the same lack of mercy.

The tabloids went hard on him. Some painted him as a fallen priest who brought shame on the Church, others hinted at guilt, as if his death was part confession, part punishment. It sold papers but it missed the point. The real story wasn't just his downfall, it was the wreckage Tobin left behind.

He destroyed lives without even being in the room. Nugent was one of them. So were the parishioners who had believed his story, the families torn apart, and the women who had survived him. Tobin's shadow stretched over everyone he touched.

When I wrote my own pieces on the story, if I had to mention the priest, I kept it simple. I didn't glorify him or damn him, I just said what was true, he was a man who lost his faith in God and in himself. Angelika's death broke him, and in the end, he couldn't live with what he knew.

By the time Father Nugent died, I was already digging. The trial had answered one question but left a hundred more. I couldn't let it go. I had files and notes stacked on my desk, names of women who had lived to tell the tale. I had started to map Tobin's movements, following the trail from Glasgow back through Brighton, Bathgate, Havant, and Margate.

I knew Nugent's death wasn't the end of anything, it was another ripple in a story that kept spreading outward.

Behind the scenes, detectives were beginning to ask the same questions I was. They wanted to know where Tobin had been, who he had lived with, who had vanished while he was around. They were linking names, dates, and disappearances and I didn't know it yet, but Operation Anagram was taking shape.

For me, it wasn't about the next scoop anymore, it was about the women whose names had been forgotten. The ones who disappeared long before Angelika, the ones who never came home. I had spent my career chasing killers, but this time it felt different. This time I was chasing ghosts.

The years that followed were messy. Tobin was locked away, but the damage he had done kept spilling out. His name became shorthand for evil in every newsroom. There were documentaries, retrospectives, endless speculation about how many victims there really were.

Cathy and I parted ways not long after the trial. I introduced her to my friend and sometime rival journalist, Marcello Mega. Cello, as everyone knew him, handled a lot of human-interest stories for magazines, the kind of work I couldn't do as staff at the *Sunday Mail*. He helped Cathy tell her story on her own terms. She had done her part with me and the paper and wanted to move on. Daniel was older now, building a new life. I didn't blame them for keeping their distance. For them it wasn't history, it was lived experience.

Sometimes I wondered if Tobin followed the coverage from his cell, if he enjoyed knowing he still had the power to keep people talking. Men like him feed off attention, it's a kind of currency.

Father Nugent was gone, Angelika was gone, and Tobin was locked up for life. On paper, that should have been the end. But I couldn't shake the feeling it wasn't. Every story, every tip, every whisper about a missing girl sent me back to my notes. I knew there were still names we didn't know. Still mothers waiting for answers. It wasn't over. Not for me.

CHAPTER FOURTEEN

THE MISSED CHANCE

OCTOBER 2005

Paisley was cloudy that night. The October chill was settling in, folk had their heads down and were heading for home and warmth. He was standing near the shop doorway, hands in his pockets, a man she had seen plenty of times before. People in the neighbourhood knew the face. He stopped to chat often enough, a quiet man who always seemed to be hanging about. He smiled when he saw her.

"Pat," he said when she asked his name. "Pat McLaughlin."

They spoke about nothing much: the weather, the football, the buses. He asked if she wanted to come in for a coffee. She hesitated, then thought there was no harm in it. It was early evening, still light, plenty of people around. The flat was on the ground floor. The smell hit her first, stale smoke, damp wet clothes, something sour underneath. The curtains were half closed. A kettle sat cold on the counter. He offered her a seat. She perched on the edge of the couch, holding her bag on her knees.

For a few minutes he was polite, then he went quiet and she felt the mood change before she understood it.

"I should get going," she said.

He turned quickly, blocking her path, the look on his face empty. He shoved her back onto the couch, his hand clamped around her throat, strong and deliberate.

She tried to shout but the sound came out like a squeak. He reached for his belt and tried to tie her wrists. When she pulled free he grabbed a bread knife from the table and the blade touched her skin just below the chin.

"Don't move," he said.

For a second she froze. Then she fought. She caught the blade with her hands and yanked it away, pain flaring through her palms, but it was enough. She pushed him, twisted, kicked at his knee and scrambled for the door.

Outside, the cold air hit her lungs and she ran barefoot along the pavement, blood streaking the slabs, shouting for help. A neighbour came out and pulled her into their hallway. Someone dialled 999.

The police came that night. She told them his name, his address, what he had tried to do. They wrote it all down. One of them said they would go straight to the flat.

They didn't.

By the time they went the next day, the door was open and the place was empty.

The knife lay on the floor beside a cushion dark with blood. The forensic team took samples, lifted fingerprints, bagged what they found.

THE MISSED CHANCE

The DNA match came back quickly. The name was already on the national database.

Peter Tobin.

He was a registered sex offender, listed after a conviction at Winchester Crown Court in 1994 for raping and assaulting two 14-year-old girls in Hampshire. He had threatened one with a knife and forced both to take pills before attacking them. The detectives in Paisley knew what that meant. They issued a warrant and began enquiries, but there was no trace. He was gone. Weeks turned into months and the file was passed from one officer to another. No national alert was issued, no photograph released. She tried to get on with her life. The cuts on her hands healed but her sleep never did. She checked the locks twice, kept the curtains shut, and avoided that street. Every few weeks she phoned the station, there was still no news.

Almost a year later she saw him again.

The television was on in the living room, the news showing police outside a church in Glasgow. Reporters were talking about a missing Polish student called Angelika Kluk. The picture changed, and there he was. The same eyes. The same face.

Her mug slipped from her hand and smashed on the floor.

Later that night she told a journalist, "I went to the police. They waited a day before going to his house. By then he'd vanished. Now an innocent girl is dead."

She was right.

If the warrant had been acted on that night, Peter Tobin would never have reached Glasgow. The name Pat McLaughlin would never have appeared on the sign-in sheet at St Patrick's Church.

At the time, nobody else understood how much had been missed. But in the months ahead detectives would reopen the Paisley file and realise that this single failure was the start of something much bigger.

The story broke in the *News of the World* first.

Across Britain, people opened their papers and read the words of a young woman from Paisley who had fought for her life and survived. Her name was printed in bold type, the photographs stark.

She told how a man calling himself Pat McLaughlin invited her into his flat for coffee, then turned violent, pinned her to the couch, and pressed a bread knife to her throat. Police had taken her statement that night, she said.

They knew his name.

They knew his address.

They promised to go straight there.

But they waited until morning.

By the time they arrived he was gone.

The paper quoted her again:

"They waited a day before going to his house. By then he'd vanished. Now an innocent girl is dead."

The connection was instant. Peter Tobin, the man arrested for the murder of Angelika Kluk.

Inside Strathclyde Police the phones started early that morning and duty officers called senior ranks at home. Copies of the article were faxed and passed hand to hand. The tone was one of disbelief. The Paisley assault file existed, the warrant was signed, and yet the suspect had not been caught.

THE MISSED CHANCE

He simply disappeared, and a year later another woman was dead.

By mid-week the force opened an internal review. The paperwork came out of storage, brown folders stacked on a long table at headquarters. Statements, forensics, photographs of the flat. Every detail confirmed what the article had said.

Officers had attended the scene, taken evidence, identified the suspect, and issued a warrant. Then the shift ended. The next team waited for daylight and when they returned, he had gone.

On the record, officials called it an unfortunate delay. Privately, detectives called it unforgivable. A known sex offender was allowed to vanish.

The file on Tobin's past read like a criminal history of post-war Britain – 32 convictions in total, the first at age 15: theft by opening lockfast place (a secured area) in Paisley, fined two pounds. Dozens more followed, housebreakings, forgeries, frauds, car thefts, assaults. Five convictions for deception and fraud between 1965 and 1984. Four offences involving police or prison authorities. Thirteen aliases. Six birth dates.

He had lived as Peter Wilson, James Kelly, Pat McLaughlin, and others the system could barely track. Every time the law closed in, he changed his name, found a new address, and started again.

In 2005 he was on the sex-offenders register for the rape of the two 14-year-old girls in Hampshire, a case that had earned him 14 years in prison. He had served his time, moved north, and was supposed to be monitored.

He wasn't.

In theory, such a man could not simply disappear. The United Kingdom's police forces were linked by a computer system known as HOLMES 2 – the Home Office Large Major Enquiry System.

It was created in the wake of the Yorkshire Ripper investigation, designed to stop killers slipping through gaps between forces. Each major incident room had a team of typists and analysts who entered every statement, name, vehicle, and address into the database. If a suspect appeared elsewhere, the system was meant to recognise him by cross-checking details such as birth date, handwriting samples, or known associates. It could compare phonetic spellings of surnames, match partial addresses, and flag overlaps between cases. But HOLMES 2 was only as strong as the information fed into it.

Each police force controlled its own data. Entries were typed manually from handwritten reports, sometimes days or weeks after an arrest. Access between regions required authorisation and some older records had never been digitised at all.

When the Paisley investigation began, Tobin's full history existed only in fragments. His Hampshire conviction sat on an old local database still awaiting upload. Strathclyde officers searching for "Pat McLaughlin" found nothing serious attached to the name. A manual check might have revealed more, but with no national trigger, the search stopped at the border. The system built to prevent another national failure had produced one of its own.

Public anger followed fast. Newspapers questioned how a

THE MISSED CHANCE

convicted rapist under supervision could vanish for nearly a year without trace. Politicians called for a review of the way high-risk offenders were tracked between England and Scotland.

The *News of the World* ran follow-ups quoting unnamed police sources who admitted "serious concern". Other papers soon took up the story and editorials used words such as 'shameful', 'avoidable', 'inexcusable. Television crews filmed outside police headquarters as senior officers promised a full inquiry.

Inside the force the mood was grim. The phrase 'missed opportunity' appeared in the internal report, but everyone understood what it really meant.

The woman in Paisley survived by luck and instinct.

Angelika Kluk did not.

That failure was now public record.

Detective Superintendent David Swindle, head of the Public Protection Unit, read the review with quiet fury. He was not known for grandstanding or noise and colleagues described him as measured, meticulous, the sort of officer who preferred method to impulse. What he saw in those pages was not a single mistake but decades of fragmentation.

He asked for Tobin's full criminal history. The printout was metres long. Every address, every alias, every offence: Bathgate, Brighton, Portsmouth, Havant, Margate, Glasgow. He spread them across his desk, tracing lines with a pen. The pattern was unmistakable, wherever Tobin lived, someone went missing or was attacked

Swindle later said it was the Paisley case that convinced him Tobin had killed before.

"The age, the method, the control," he recalled. "It all pointed to a man who'd done this before."

He began to assemble a small analytical team within Strathclyde Police. Their first task was to reconstruct Tobin's life, year by year, and identify every known alias and address. They would then cross-check those movements against missing-person cases held by other forces.

To do that, Swindle needed cooperation beyond Scotland. He contacted Hampshire, Sussex, Kent, and Essex. He asked for access to their databases, for photocopies of old files, for any outstanding cases that might overlap with Tobin's timeline. Swindle wanted to build what the official systems had never achieved: a single, coherent picture of one man's criminal life.

The work began quietly in the final weeks of 2006. There were no press releases or briefings, only requests and late-night phone calls between police forces across the UK. Boxes of files arrived from other forces, marked Historic Enquiries and To Be Indexed. Analysts entered the details manually into HOLMES 2, creating a new master record under the name Peter Tobin.

For the first time, every alias pointed back to a single person.

By Christmas the outline was complete. A lifetime of movement, from Paisley to the south coast and back again. Dozens of temporary jobs, rented rooms, and false identities. Swindle showed the map to senior officers — red pins for addresses, yellow for victims. The board looked like a crime atlas of Britain.

It was then he made his proposal.

What they needed, he said, was not another murder inquiry

but a national operation dedicated to one man. It would unite every police force touched by his history. It would gather every address, every alias, every missing woman, every scrap of evidence that might still be sitting in an archive.

He called it Operation Anagram. The name reflected the puzzle they faced: letters, dates, and identities that had to be rearranged until they made sense.

Senior officers, perhaps sensing a way of quelling the public mistrust, approved the plan early in 2007. The public never saw the internal memos that authorised it, but the logic was simple.

A single failure in Paisley had exposed a weakness that ran through the entire system.

If they could fix that, maybe they could find every woman who had ever crossed his path.

The review ended not with blame but with resolve. For those who read the file, there was no doubt, Peter Tobin had slipped through the cracks of British policing.

Operation Anagram would be the attempt to close them.

CHAPTER FIFTEEN

THE BIRTH OF OPERATION ANAGRAM

IN THE MONTHS after the Kluk trial, Detective Superintendent David Swindle began looking backwards instead of forwards.

He set up Operation Anagram at the same time as running the Angelika Kluk murder investigation but kept it confidential for fear of adverse pre-trial publicity.

What first made him look twice at Tobin's past wasn't gossip or coincidence.

"The extent of the injuries, his conduct after the crime, how organised he was, the aliases, the travelling. My intuition and professional judgement told me there was more," he said.

Within weeks, a covert operation began to quietly map Tobin's movements, from addresses and vehicles to jobs and aliases.

At the start of 2007 a few police officers gathered in an office at Strathclyde Police Headquarters. On paper their task seemed simple – trace every year of Peter Tobin's life, map his movements and trace anyone who may have crossed his path. In practice, it was a near impossible task. Det Supt David Swindle

THE BIRTH OF OPERATION ANAGRAM

ran it himself. He'd spent years in major crime and knew what it meant to start with only scraps of information. The walls were covered in maps of Britain, the kind you would see in a classroom, and they marked out every town Tobin ever passed through, every place a woman had gone missing.

Over the next few months those maps became dense with red and yellow pins. Every new discovery made the map darker.

The name Anagram had come to Swindle while looking at a list of aliases. Peter Tobin had lived as Peter Wilson, Pat McLaughlin, James Kelly, and a dozen others.

Each new identity was another rearrangement of the same man, another chance to vanish into ordinary life. The operation would do the opposite: take those scrambled pieces and set them back in order.

The work was slow. Investigators began by pulling all known convictions and prison records.

Then came tenancy forms, employment histories, vehicle registrations, hospital visits, and driving licences.

Everything went into HOLMES 2, the same system that had failed to link the Paisley assault.

This time it was used differently.

Every alias, every spelling variation, every possible date of birth was entered and cross-checked. For the first time, the machine was fed his entire history rather than fragments of it.

The first clear pattern emerged in spring.

Analysts noticed Tobin had lived at an address in Bathgate, West Lothian, in early 1991.

It was the same town where 15-year-old Vicky Hamilton

vanished that February while waiting for a bus home to Redding after visiting her sister.

The coincidence was too sharp to ignore.

Swindle authorised a team to re-examine the old case files.

The girl's family had waited 16 years for an answer, now they finally had a reason to hope. Forensic officers searched the Bathgate property where Tobin once lived and in the loft they found a five-inch knife, rusted and hidden behind insulation. Tests confirmed it was Vicky's DNA on the blade. It was the first physical link between Tobin and a missing person other than Angelika Kluk.

Swindle's hunch had been right, this was not one man who killed once; this was a pattern stretching back decades.

The discovery transformed the operation overnight and what began as a speculative audit became a national manhunt.

Swindle briefed his superiors, and the call went out to every police force that had ever held a file on Tobin. Hampshire, Sussex, Kent, Essex, Dorset, Cheshire, Staffordshire, Surrey, the Metropolitan Police – all were asked to send information north.

The number of detectives assigned to Anagram doubled and a dedicated incident room was set up at Pitt Street. Walls disappeared under maps and case charts. Boxes of possible evidence arrived daily, some marked with dates from the 1960s and 70s.

Swindle spoke rarely to the media during those months, but when he did, his message was clear.

"We are looking at every aspect of this man's life," he said. "It's about giving answers to families."

THE BIRTH OF OPERATION ANAGRAM

Behind those calm words, his office was working around the clock and in November 2007, another breakthrough came.

During the review of Tobin's Bathgate tenancy, detectives found he had moved to a house in Margate, Kent, soon after Vicky Hamilton disappeared.

Neighbours there remembered him digging in the garden, always at night, never planting anything. The information was passed to Kent Police and a search warrant was granted for 50 Irvine Drive. Forensic teams began excavating the garden and within days they found what they had been looking for. Beneath the patio, wrapped in plastic, lay the remains of a young girl.

But they were stunned when they realised the garden grave held another secret. Further excavation uncovered a second body a few feet away.

The first was confirmed as Vicky Hamilton and on 21 July 2007, Tobin was formally charged with her murder.

The second, identified through dental records, was 18-year-old Dinah McNicol, a student from Essex who vanished after hitchhiking home from a music festival in 1991.

The news hit every front page in Britain.

Finally, 16 years after both girls disappeared, the same man was linked to their deaths.

Tobin transported Vicky's body from Scotland to England, hid it in his new garden, and later buried Dinah beside her.

It was proof of a level of calculation and control that chilled even experienced detectives.

One officer described it as "the moment everything changed".

At Strathclyde headquarters, Swindle stood in front of the

wall map again. Two red pins now marked the length of the country – Bathgate and Margate – joined by a single black line. It had taken a long time to connect them.

After the discovery in Margate, the machinery of Anagram shifted into national gear. Meetings were held between senior officers from 10 police forces. They compared unsolved cases, missing-person lists, and travel histories and dozens of old files were reopened.

The question was now no longer whether Tobin had killed again but how many times.

In December 2007, 40 of Britain's top detectives met in Glasgow for what journalists later called the Tobin Summit. It was chaired by Hampshire Assistant Chief Constable Steve Watts, who formally oversaw Operation Anagram at national level.

Swindle briefed them in person.

He laid out the evidence: the Bathgate knife, 20 items of jewellery found in the same loft, DNA from five unidentified females on those objects, and a timeline covering more than 40 years.

He told them there were still gaps in the chronology, missing months and years that had to be filled.

The plan was to build a single national profile of Tobin's movements from 1962 to the present day.

The scale of the work was unprecedented and each participating force appointed liaison officers to feed their information into HOLMES 2.

By early 2008, Operation Anagram had generated more than 1,000 active lines of inquiry.

THE BIRTH OF OPERATION ANAGRAM

The jewellery recovered from the Bathgate loft became a focus of public appeal.

Sapphire rings, crucifixes, watches, a St Christopher medal, bracelets. Police released photographs, asking anyone who recognised them to come forward. Each item was treated as potential evidence of another victim. To this day, none has ever been claimed.

The traces of DNA from five unidentified women found on the pieces hinted at more potential deaths.

Swindle refused to speculate publicly about numbers and kept the focus on the women they could name: Angelika, Vicky, Dinah.

Behind the scenes, he urged his team to keep searching, he believed there were others.

On 16 November 2007, Tobin was formally charged with the murder of Dinah McNicol.

He would be back in court the following year.

But first, it was time for the end of Vicky's story to be heard at last.

CHAPTER SIXTEEN

BACK IN THE DOCK

PETER TOBIN'S NAME had become shorthand for everything people feared. The killing of Angelika Kluk made him a national obsession. When police began linking him to cold cases, the story took on a different shape. The story was no longer about a single murder, but about the fear there might be more.

The High Court in Dundee was the centre of the nation's attention in November 2008. It was already full before the doors opened to the public. Police stood at every entrance.

The press waited in silence, notebooks ready, outside the photographers had their cameras ready to capture the families and, hopefully, images of Tobin arriving in the prison van. Finally, 16 years after Vicky Hamilton vanished, the man accused of killing her was about to face a jury.

The courtroom filled quickly. Detectives, lawyers, and members of the public took their seats. At the front sat Michael Hamilton, the father of the girl whose face had once filled every newspaper in Scotland.

BACK IN THE DOCK

WEEK ONE

Peter Tobin was brought into the dock just before 10am. He was smaller than people expected, grey-haired and hunched, his movements slow. When he sat down, he barely looked up. The clerk read out the charges. Abduction. Rape. Murder. Each word hung in the air.

Advocate Depute Alex Prentice spoke first and told the jury that this was not just a case about a missing girl, but about a man who lived behind false names for decades.

He laid out the broad shape of what they would hear: how Vicky was taken in 1991, how her body was found 16 years later buried under a patio in Kent, and how evidence from two homes, 400 miles apart, had brought the truth to light.

Among the first police witnesses was a Bathgate constable who had been a young officer back in 1991 when Vicky was first reported missing. In the witness box he described the early door-to-door enquiries, bus routes checked, shopfronts visited, and the routine sweep of the streets where she was last seen. Nothing stood out. A man answered one of the doors, spoke briefly, and the house was logged as checked and cleared.

Sixteen years later police returned to that same address, this time in protective overalls during the renewed search. They were there when the loft hatch was opened and the insulation pulled back. Beneath the old insulation they recovered a knife later found to carry tissue and DNA evidence consistent with Vicky Hamilton. It was one of the discoveries that linked the house in Bathgate to the grave in Margate and began to close the 16-year gap in the case.

WEEK TWO

The second week opened with scientists from the Scottish Police Services Authority, known at the time as the SPSA.

Before the forensic evidence began, the Advocate Depute explained that the scientific work in the case had been carried out by them. It was a national body set up to support Scotland's police forces with shared services such as fingerprint analysis, DNA profiling and forensic science.

The SPSA's laboratories handled crime scene evidence from across the country, testing samples and reporting their findings to the Crown Office and Procurator Fiscal Service.

Their scientists worked independently from the investigating officers and followed a strict chain of custody rules, meaning every item, from a knife to a single fibre, was tracked, labelled and signed for at each stage of testing.

Forensic scientists took the jury through the physical evidence that had survived since 1991. They explained how trace fibres found with Vicky's remains were consistent with materials from Tobin's former home in Bathgate, and they outlined the limited DNA that could still be recovered after so many years. They emphasised their job was not to suggest guilt or innocence, only to lay out the science.

The jury listened closely, most taking notes.

The court heard how Tobin lived under another name, how

he had rented the Bathgate house, and how, within weeks of Vicky's disappearance, he moved south to Margate. The evidence was laid out step by step.

Then came the testimony of Cathy Wilson – giving evidence against Tobin for the second time. She told the court how she had lived with Tobin during the early 1990s. She spoke quietly, describing his temper, his sudden disappearances, the fear that grew around him. She confirmed that he had moved from Bathgate to Margate that same year.

That week, Tobin sat almost motionless. He avoided looking at the witnesses and sometimes appeared to close his eyes when photographs were shown.

The Crown's case was building a simple but devastating line: she had been taken, murdered, and later transported to England.

What came next would be about the wider pattern, the places he'd lived, the names he'd used, and the trail he left behind.

WEEK THREE

By the third week of the trial, the atmosphere inside the Dundee High Court had changed. The reporters still filled the benches and the public still turned up. Everyone knew the case was now about evidence. Not theories, not arguments, just proof.

Forensic officers who searched the Bathgate house gave evidence. They described the search in plain detail. The loft had been full of dust and insulation, the kind that sticks to your skin and clothes. Among the debris they found a rusted knife and a small box containing pieces of jewellery. Each item was photographed, sealed, and logged before being taken away for testing.

The courtroom was silent as they explained the process, how the chain of evidence had been maintained since the first recovery.

The years had passed, but the proof remained intact. On screens, photographs of the Bathgate loft were shown. The jurors leaned forward. There was nothing dramatic in the pictures, just insulation and old timber, yet everyone understood what it meant.

Next came the forensic archaeologists from Kent Police who supervised the excavation in Margate. They spoke about the patio that had been laid over the garden and how it had been lifted piece by piece. Beneath the concrete slabs was a shallow grave lined with plastic sheeting. Inside were the remains of a young girl.

The officer said that when they began to clear the soil further along the same trench, they found a second package. It was smaller but wrapped the same way. That moment changed the entire investigation. The pathologist confirmed what the detectives had already suspected. The first remains were later identified as Vicky Hamilton. The second would later be confirmed as Dinah McNicol. The coincidence was impossible to ignore.

The jury heard how Tobin had rented the house in Margate, built a new patio, and carried on as if nothing had happened. The analysts explained the timing. Vicky disappeared in

February 1991, Tobin moved in March. The Crown's case was that he transported her body across the country and buried her in his new garden.

The analysts who reconstructed Tobin's movements were called after that. They presented his timeline in a way that made the scale of his life visible. Every known address, job, and alias appeared on a screen in front of the jury. Bathgate. Havant. Portsmouth. Brighton. Margate. Glasgow. A line joined them across the map of Britain.

They explained how they had pieced it together from tenancy forms, employment records, vehicle registrations, and old police statements.

They said Tobin had used at least at least a dozen known aliases and dozens of addresses since the 1960s. Each time he was questioned by police or employers, the name changed. It was a pattern of movement designed to erase his trail.

When the analysts finished, the courtroom was quiet. Even the defence team sat still, their pens resting on the table. The scale of it all was too large to dismiss.

The following witnesses were from the family. They spoke softly, describing Vicky as she had been before the headlines. A teenager with a quick laugh, proud of her hair, full of plans. Her father, Michael, had waited 16 years to hear her name spoken in a courtroom. He kept his eyes fixed on the floor as her belongings were shown one by one.

There were small things that carried unbearable weight. A purse, a photograph, a school notebook. The evidence officers laid them out carefully under the bright lights. When the day ended, people filed out in silence, even the reporters said little. Outside, the light was already fading.

The trial was not finished, but the story had already been told in full. Every new witness only confirmed what everyone in that room already knew.

WEEK FOUR

By the fourth week, the trial was almost over. The jurors arrived early, faces pale with fatigue. The court clerks moved quietly between the benches and reporters took their usual places, their notebooks already open. The crowds that had packed the first days were thinning now. The interest hadn't gone, but the shock had dulled and they got the proceedings from the press.

Forensic experts described how Vicky's remains were found buried in the garden at 50 Irvine Drive in Margate, wrapped inside black plastic bags and covered with a layer of concrete and soil. Other forensic findings included bruising and traces of the sedative amitriptyline were identified during post-mortem examination. Taken together, the evidence showed she had been violently assaulted and concealed shortly after her disappearance in 1991, when Tobin left Bathgate for Margate.

When the final witness stepped down, the courtroom seemed to exhale. Months of investigation had been distilled into four weeks of testimony. What remained were the arguments.

Alex Prentice QC rose first for the Crown. He reminded the jury of what they had seen: the evidence from Bathgate, the knife, the DNA, the witness statements that had placed Tobin there at the right time.

He said the case was not about speculation but about facts that had waited 16 years to be seen.

When he sat down, the silence held for a moment before Donald Finclay KC stood for the defence. He reminded the jury of the time that had passed, the fallibility of memory, the risk of drawing conclusions from fragments. He told them that doubt was not a weakness, that the burden lay entirely with the Crown. He spoke without notes, pacing slowly as he talked. He had done this many times before and knew how to hold a room.

When the jury retired, the Hamilton family stayed seated, quiet and still, and after three hours, word came that the jury were ready.

Inside, everyone stood as they filed back into the courtroom. The clerk asked the question and the foreman gave the answer. Guilty of abduction. Guilty of rape. Guilty of murder.

Tobin did not move. He kept his head down, hands clasped in front of him.

From the public benches came a sound that was part relief, part grief. Vicky's sister Sharon stood outside the court later and faced the cameras.

Her voice shook but her words were clear.

"At least now we know," she said. "It's taken 16 years to bring her home."

Behind her, detectives stood quietly. Some nodded, some looked away. They had lived this case for years, through dead ends and false leads, now it was finished.

In Redding, people left flowers at the small memorial stone bearing Vicky's name. In Bathgate, neighbours who had once ignored the old address stopped and stared at it when they passed. The headlines spoke of justice and closure, but those closest to it knew there was no such thing.

After the trial ended, Tobin was sentenced immediately.

You could feel the tension in the air.

Lord Emslie looked directly at him as he began. He said Tobin was "unfit to live in a decent society".

He spoke of Vicky as a vulnerable teenager who had needed help on her way home and instead fell into his clutches. Her short life, he said, ended in a disgusting and degrading way. He told Tobin that it was hard to convey the loathing and revulsion ordinary people would feel for what he had done.

The judge sentenced him to life imprisonment with a minimum term of 30 years, which replaced the minimum term he was already serving for the murder of Angelika Kluk. This ensured he would not be eligible for release for at least 30 years.

The calculation made the message clear, he would never be released.

Tobin stared at the floor while the sentence was read and said nothing. The guards led him out, his head low, the same way he had left every courtroom before.

Outside, Michael and Sharon Hamilton spoke briefly. They said justice had come too late for their mother, but at least the truth was known. They hoped people would remember Vicky as she was, not for what had been done to her. Around them, strangers clapped. Police officers shook hands with them. The family left through a side door, heads down against the flashbulbs. That night the television news replayed their words again and again. People lit candles in Redding and Falkirk and for once, the public grief felt united.

When the doors of Dundee High Court finally closed, the sound of the lock echoed in the hall. It marked the end of one story and the start of another that was still to come.

Once the sentencing was done, the benches were already being cleared for the next trial. The cables were coiled, the lights switched off. For everyone else it was over, another story finished. For the Hamilton family, it wasn't peace but it was an ending of sorts. For the family there could never be closure.

**

That winter, the city felt tense. Every newsstand carried Tobin's face. 'Monster in the Dock'. 'Killer Dad of Three'. The coverage grew darker each day. People wanted to understand how a man could live among them, move from parish to parish, and go unseen. Radio phone-ins filled with fury. Some callers compared him to Bible John, the infamous Glasgow serial killer suspected of killing three women in the 1960s. Others said he was worse.

CHAPTER SEVENTEEN

THE FINAL TRIAL

BY THE WINTER of 2009, Peter Tobin was a familiar figure in courtrooms across Britain. Two murder convictions had already been secured against him, but the investigations into his past did not close. Detectives were still working through the long years he spent moving from city to city, changing names, and slipping through gaps. One of those gaps held the story of an 18-year-old girl who vanished in 1991. Her name was Dinah McNicol.

When Dinah's remains were finally found in 2007, detectives in Kent and Scotland knew immediately her story would no longer sit unanswered. What remained was damaged by time but still strong enough to bring a case to court. Nearly 18 years had passed since she was last seen alive. Whatever had happened to her would now have to be presented to a jury.

The legal route to that moment would be a long process. The Crown Prosecution Service served a summons on Tobin in September 2008, accusing him of Dinah's murder.

A trial was fixed for June 2009 at Chelmsford Crown Court. That first hearing opened with the prosecution laying out the essential evidence they relied upon. They described Dinah's disappearance, the circumstances of the lift she accepted with her friend David Tremlett, and the discovery of her body in Margate, buried close to the remains of Vicky Hamilton.

But the June proceedings never reached a verdict.

Within two weeks, the judge ruled that Tobin was unfit to continue pending treatment for a heart problem. This resulted in the jury being discharged and the trial collapsing.

Dinah's family, who had already waited almost two decades, were told they would have to wait again. Everything would need to be restarted when Tobin was well enough to stand trial.

A new date was set for December 2009 and this time, the case ran its full course.

On the morning of 14 December, Tobin was brought back to Chelmsford Crown Court. Reporters gathered, but the scene was nothing like Glasgow or Dundee. There were no crowds outside, no sense of spectacle and the atmosphere felt stripped down. Dinah's family arrived, taking their seats inside the public gallery. Detectives from the various forces involved in Operation Anagram were present too, sitting among members of the public who had followed the earlier trials.

DAY ONE – 14 DECEMBER 2009

When the court rose, and Tobin was led into the dock, he moved the same way he always did. His head was lowered, and he listened through an earpiece. He wore a dark shirt and trousers. His posture was hunched, and he kept his gaze fixed on the floor. Four prison officers stood near him throughout the hearing. A short distance away sat Ian McNicol, Dinah's father, surrounded by relatives.

The clerk read out the charge of murder. Tobin gave no response. He barely lifted his head. The jury of 12 was sworn in, and the prosecution began setting out the core details of the case.

The prosecution relied heavily on the evidential framework presented during the first trial that collapsed. The jurors were told that in August 1991, Dinah had been hitchhiking home from a music festival in Liphook, Hampshire. She and a man she had met at the festival, David Tremlett, were picked up on the A3 by a driver in what was described at the time as an old, scruffy car. The driver dropped Tremlett off at Junction 8 of the M25. Dinah continued alone with the man behind the wheel. She was not seen alive again.

The Crown told the jury that, at the time of her disappearance, Tobin was living in Margate. He regularly travelled between Margate and Portsmouth to collect and return his young son from Cathy Wilson, his estranged wife. His weekend journeys took him directly past the A3, the Liphook area and Junction 8, the same route Dinah had taken.

The jury was told what happened two years earlier. In November 2007, police began searching the garden of 50 Irvine Drive, Margate, a house Tobin once lived in. During the excavation, officers uncovered two sets of remains. One was identified as Vicky Hamilton. The other was Dinah McNicol. Both had been wrapped in multiple layers of refuse bags. Dinah were bound and gagged. Her body was found in a shallow grave and covered with concrete.

Photographs taken during the 2007 excavation were shown in court. They showed the slabs lifted and stacked, the soil removed in sections and the plastic bundles being uncovered. The images were stark, and the courtroom fell completely silent as the sequence was displayed.

Expert evidence showed that Tobin's fingerprints had been recovered from three of the refuse sacks used to wrap Dinah's remains. Toxicology evidence confirmed that her body contained amitriptyine, a sedative, as well as traces of the sleeping pill triazolam and cannabis. The jury heard Tobin had previously used sedative drugs on two schoolgirls in 1994. They also heard that in April 1990, he had been treated in hospital after taking an overdose of triazolam. The prosecution argued that the evidence was consistent with Dinah having been drugged before her death.

The court was also told about the account of David Martin, a neighbour in Irvine Drive in 1991. He had seen Tobin digging a deep hole in his garden during the summer months. When he asked what it was for, Tobin claimed it was a sandpit for his son. Their conversation was joking and light-hearted. Martin remembered it because he made a joke asking if Tobin was 'going for Australia' such was the depth.

A few days later, when the hole was filled, Tobin told him social services had objected. Checks later showed no record of any such intervention. Throughout the first day, Dinah's family listened in silence. Tobin did not look up once.

DAY TWO – 15 DECEMBER 2009

The second day focused on the forensic evidence. Home Office pathologist Dr David Rouse gave detailed testimony about the discoveries made during his examinations.

He told the court that Dinah's remains were tied at the wrists and ankles, bound behind her back, gagged with a knotted gag found in her mouth and folded tightly before being wrapped in 16 refuse sacks. Her body was then buried beneath the patio. The pathologist explained that her clothing and jewellery, along with DNA analysis, helped confirm her identity.

He stated there was no evidence of sexual assault available to him because of the level of decomposition and that any such injuries would be extremely hard to identify after 16 years. In Vicky Hamilton's case, enough soft tissue remained for forensic examination. The distinction lay in the condition of the bodies, not the nature of the crimes. The cause of death was unascertained but consistent with ligature strangulation and gagging. He told the court it was likely she was dead when she was placed in the grave.

The prosecution then turned to Dinah's bank account. She had been awarded £2,700 following her mother's death in a car accident and had withdrawn only £220 of it. After her disappearance, more than £2,000 was taken from her account. The withdrawals were made in Margate, Ramsgate, Brighton, and finally Portsmouth. The Crown said those towns were places Tobin was known to frequent at that time.

Because this was an English trial, the jury was allowed to

hear parts of Tobin's criminal history under the bad character provisions of the Criminal Justice Act 2003. The judge ruled that certain earlier offences were admissible because they were relevant to specific issues in the case, including identity, intent and the way the offence had been committed.

The jury was told about Tobin's 1994 convictions for drugging and assaulting two schoolgirls, which involved the use of sedatives. They were also told about his conviction for the murder of Vicky Hamilton. The court admitted this material because the prosecution argued that the earlier conduct demonstrated a distinct pattern: targeting teenage girls, using drugs to incapacitate them, binding or restraining them and concealing their bodies in bags.

The judge directed the jury that the purpose of this evidence was limited. They could consider it only insofar as it helped them decide whether Tobin was responsible for Dinah's death, and they were warned not to convict him simply because he had behaved similarly in the past. Dinah's family stayed in their seats until the court adjourned.

DAY THREE – 16 DECEMBER 2009

The third day moved quickly. After the prosecution closed its case, Tobin's barrister, Oliver Blunt QC, stood and addressed the court.

"On behalf of Peter Tobin, we call no evidence."

There was no defence. No witnesses. No alternative account. No explanation for the fingerprint evidence or the grave. Blunt reminded the jury that Tobin's background should not obscure the requirement to be sure of guilt. He suggested that the presence of Tobin's fingerprints on the bags did not prove he had killed Dinah and raised the possibility that he had simply handled the items before someone else used them.

It was a thin argument in the face of the evidence. He sat down. The judge reminded the jury they must decide the case only on the evidence they had heard and that they had to be sure of guilt before returning a verdict. He warned them not to let emotion or Tobin's past offences influence their decision. They retired.

Everything that had taken 18 years to reach a court of law was now in their hands.

They were gone for 13 minutes.

Tobin was brought back into the dock. The foreman stood and gave the verdict aloud.

"Guilty."

There was no visible reaction from Tobin. Some members of the jury wept as more graphic details of his earlier crimes were outlined, which is permitted only after the verdict.

In the gallery, Dinah's father closed his eyes and her siblings held hands. Michael Hamilton, Vicky's father, was present for the verdict and placed a hand on Ian McNicol's shoulder. The two men exchanged a quiet nod, no words were required. They had lived with different details but suffered the same loss.

Tobin stood as Mr Justice Calvert-Smith passed sentence. He told him he had committed a terrible crime. He sentenced him to life imprisonment with a minimum term of 30 years.

THE FINAL TRIAL

That sentence was to run consecutively to what he was already serving. In practical terms, it meant it was unlikely he would ever be released. Tobin was taken down without a word.

Outside the court, Ian McNicol made a short statement. His voice was shaky but he held it together.

"After 18 long years, we can finally say goodbye to Dinah."

He thanked the detectives who had refused to give up. He thanked the members of the public who supported the search over a long period. Then he left with his family.

Inside the building, detectives involved in Operation Anagram spoke for the first time since the verdict. They called Tobin a man capable of extreme cruelty and confirmed they were still pursuing a large number of outstanding lines of inquiry. They released images of jewellery found in Tobin's possession, pieces they believed might belong to other unidentified victims. They did not pretend the work was finished, it was only moving into a different stage.

The trial of Dinah McNicol closed a chapter that had started on a road in Hampshire in 1991 and ended in a courtroom nearly two decades later. It answered the question of who was responsible for her death, but it did not answer all the questions about Peter Tobin.

***

The conviction might have closed the courtroom chapter of Dinah McNicol's case, but one voice that had hovered around the edges for nearly two decades did not surface until long after the trial was finished.

David Tremlett had been the last known person to see Dinah alive before she got into the car with the man who murdered her. His own account became public months after Tobin was convicted.

He said he had met Dinah at the Liphook festival in the summer of 1991. They had got on well from the start. They wandered around the fields together, talked about nothing in particular and everything at once, they had a sort of easy, instant connection that happens sometimes in a lifetime. When they left the festival, she chose to travel with him, leaving her friends behind. They hitched lifts, without thinking too much about it.

Tremlett remembered the driver who stopped for them. He said the man felt wrong from the beginning. He could not explain why, only that something in the man's manner made him uneasy. Dinah climbed into the front seat, Tremlett sat in the back as they drove north.

When the car reached Junction 8 of the M25, Tremlett got out. He wanted to reach his mother's house in Surrey, and this was the turning he needed. He watched the car pull away with Dinah still in the passenger seat. He later said he had tried to memorise the registration number because something about the driver did not sit right with him. That was the last moment he saw her.

When Dinah did not contact him, he called the number she had given him a few times, but there was only an answering machine. He said he did not leave a message because he assumed she might not want to talk or had moved on. He had no idea she was missing. It was months later when a friend told him she had been featured on the BBC's Crimewatch programme. He went to the police in Redhill and gave them everything he could remember about the man in the car and the journey. He said the interview was long and uncomfortable.

He was questioned closely and, for a time, felt as if the police saw him as a suspect.

Tremlett said the memory of Dinah and what happened to her never left him. He did not read newspaper reports about Dinah or watch television coverage in case he was ever asked to identify someone. He said he wanted his recollection to remain his own. In 2007, he was contacted again when the investigation reopened, and he gave a full statement.

After Tobin was convicted, he spoke publicly for the first time. He talked about the guilt that had attached itself to him. He wondered whether he should have insisted Dinah get out of the car with him, or whether they should have waited for another lift. He said he knew, logically, that he was not responsible for what happened, but the thought stayed with him anyway.

His account did not change the facts of the case. What Tremlett offered was a window into the ordinary moment where danger entered without any warning. There was nothing unusual in how their story began. A music festival, a fun weekend, the journey to get home, a stranger's car pulling up, the driver offering them a lift — something thousands of young people did without a second thought. At a motorway junction, they said goodbye, both expecting they would be home within the hour. Only one of them was. The other was swallowed by the dark and not found again for almost two decades.

The trial laid out the facts as courts must. Tremlett's words filled in the spaces around them. All he could offer was the memory of leaving and the guilt of being the one who survived.

Followed Dinah's trial was the long shadow of the appeal. Tobin lodged papers to challenge the 30-year minimum term, and for months the process dragged on. Hearings were repeatedly postponed throughout 2010 and into early 2011, often because he claimed to be unwell or simply refused to appear. For the families it felt like another round of delays.

In August 2010 the fathers of Vicky Hamilton and Dinah McNicol publicly condemned the appeal as a farce and urged that it be stopped. The process remained technically active into 2011, even preventing Vicky's belongings from being returned to her father. Eventually Tobin filed a minute of abandonment, ending the last legal manoeuvre available to him.

CHAPTER EIGHTEEN

UNFOLDING THE ANAGRAM

JUSTICE HAD COME slowly, piece by piece. It came through detectives who refused to let go and families who continued to seek answers as the years passed.

As Vicky and Dinah's families sat through those agonising trials, Operation Anagram continued to operate quietly in the background, cross-referencing every unsolved disappearance that might overlap with Tobin's timeline.

Each location was matched against old missing-person files, unsolved murders and sexual assaults dating back to the 1960s. Analysts rebuilt Tobin's life year by year and filled the gaps with anything they could find: prison logs, hospital admissions, vehicle registrations, and tenancy records. Over 100 unsolved murders and disappearances were reviewed. Forensic scientists compared fingerprints, DNA profiles and witness statements. Officers revisited old addresses.

Different regions held separate fragments of his life, none of which spoke to the others. Anagram forced those walls to come down. Meetings were held through 2008 and 2009 with senior officers from every part of the country. They compared notes, traded leads and agreed new searches. Reports went to the Association of Chief Police Officers.

They weren't the only ones who'd been taking notes…

For me, the story should have ended with Angelika's death, with one crime, one monster, one headline. But I'd spent long enough around murder to know that some names open doors instead of closing them. When I joined the *Sunday Mail* in 2004, the old building on Anderston Quay was still standing, right beside the Copycat pub. The two sat almost side by side, like extensions of the same place. The Copycat was where generations of Mail and Record reporters gathered – not just after hours, but all hours. Stories were traded over pints, tips scribbled on napkins, scoops born out of smoke and noise. Huge bar tabs were run up and put on expenses.

By the time I came along, that world was drawing to a close. I was part of the new breed – the ones who filed from laptops instead of bars, who drank coffee instead of lager, who worked from home, cars, and borrowed desks. The Copycat was still there when I started, but already part of a vanishing culture. Not long after, it and the old office were flattened, and I was working from the new glass-and-steel building at Central Quay.

The heart of the paper had shifted next door, all bright lights and security passes, but some things stayed the same. The newsroom was still full of noise and clacking keys, still fuelled by instinct. And downstairs, the library was its memory. Campbell and the other librarians who worked at the *Daily Record* and *Sunday Mail* could pull a cutting from any year in minutes.

UNFOLDING THE ANAGRAM

Before the digital archive, you went to them if you needed to remember how a story began.

They kept the past alive while the rest of us chased the present.

I started flicking through some of those old stories we had pulled, cross-checking dates and places.

It didn't feel like work, it never did in those days. Chasing a story was pure adrenaline – a rush, a natural high if you like. I always thanked my lucky stars I wasn't in just a job, I was doing something I loved.

Instinct drew me towards the old cuttings, old stories that had happened before my time. I felt a familiar itch – the same that had pulled me through a hundred other nights.

Somewhere, I thought, there will be more.

I typed his name into the system and began plotting the dots I could find: the cities and towns we knew he had lived or passed through. The list looked like the itinerary of a man who couldn't stay still.

Every one of those towns had its own ghosts – women who had vanished without trace, murders filed away under "unsolved".

I began matching the years.

In 1974 he was believed to be in East Anglia. In 1980, Brighton. In 1988, he'd drifted between the south coast and Scotland, leaving wreckage in his wake. I pulled out a notebook where I'd scribbled names during other investigations.

Some I'd written off, but now they jumped out at me: Jessie Earl. Louise Kay. Pamela Exall. All from the south coast. All young, all gone. Cases that had never been solved.

I told myself I was being ridiculous. Who did I think I was –

one reporter sitting in her living room, trying to solve half the country's cold cases? But I kept going.

Because somewhere between instinct and obsession, you lose the ability to walk away. I wanted something to take to my bosses and for it to be a story they would be immersed in as much as I was. Tobin was a serial killer, I could feel it in my bones. I remembered a detective once telling me that the best killers learn to hide in the ordinary. They blend.

The most dangerous men don't draw attention to themselves, they slip through ordinary life unnoticed. Tobin had done that for decades.

While the police were building their official timeline in Operation Anagram, I was building mine.

My desk was chaos – notes covered in pencil circles, Post-its layered three deep, printouts of photographs I could barely look at and old stories.

One of my old police contacts called to say quietly, "You're not daft, Jane. There's more to him." He didn't need to convince me.

A few years before, after developing a fascination for unsolved cases while I was crime reporter at the *Edinburgh Evening News*, I'd started a file that would follow me for years – a folder I labelled Unsolved.

As I flicked through my little folder, I couldn't help but wonder if some of them were his? During my investigations into Tobin, my folder had acquired some English cases too.

***

Then I traced Tobin's old addresses, the same pattern kept appearing along the south coast.

He drifted through seaside towns, working odd jobs, moving on before anyone noticed. In each one, a woman had disappeared.

Some cases were famous. Others barely made it beyond the local paper.

But when I laid them against his timeline, they began to tell a very similar and worrying story.

JESSIE EARL, EASTBOURNE, 1980

Jessie's file was one of the first I pulled. She was 22 and came from Eastbourne. An art and design student who kept to herself. Friends said she was shy, thoughtful, sometimes unsure of her place in the world. She liked to draw, to listen more than speak. Nothing about her stood out.

She vanished in May 1980. Her parents initially believed she had gone away for the weekend. When she did not return, she was reported missing.

Nine years later, walkers found her remains in the scrub near Beachy Head. Naked, her hands tied with her own bra. The police couldn't say exactly when she'd died.

I didn't see the photographs, but the reports were enough. The language of violence is always the same. The binding. The isolation. The need to control and humiliate.

It was a pattern I recognised. The same hallmarks that would appear in Tobin's known victims. He was living in Brighton then, about 30 miles from where Jessie disappeared. Working casual jobs, moving between digs, using different names. Detectives on Operation Anagram later confirmed her case had been reviewed.

One of them told me, "It's not proof, Jane, but it's close. The geography and the method fit him like a glove." But there was no DNA. No eyewitnesses. No confession. So Jessie's file went back on the shelf. Reopened, re-examined, still unresolved.

LOUISE KAY, EASTBOURNE, 1988

Jessie's case had raised questions. Louise Kay's disappearance raised more. She was 18. Bright, funny, independent.

On the night she vanished, 23 June 1988, she was out with friends at the Kings Country Club near Eastbourne. She left around 3am, saying she planned to sleep in her gold Fiesta parked nearby. She was never seen again and the car was never found.

By then Tobin was living in Brighton under another name, working as a handyman and occasional driver. Later he moved to Crawley. He had access to houses under renovation and vehicles that came and went.

Years later police searched one of the properties he had worked on, believing the car could have been hidden under concrete. Nothing was found, but the question never went away.

Her case was later reviewed by Operation Anagram. Detectives noted the timing, the geography, the circumstance. It all pointed the same way. There was no proof, only the pattern.

If Tobin had claimed another life in England, Louise Kay was the name most often mentioned.

PAMELA EXALL, NORFOLK, 1974

Pamela's story is older and almost forgotten. She was 22, working in a seaside village in Norfolk, when she vanished walking home from a pub in 1974.

It was a warm night. She told friends she would take the shortcut along the coastal road. Her handbag was found near a caravan site. She never made it home.

Tobin was in East Anglia that year, moving between labouring jobs and using early aliases. Police later learned he had done seasonal work not far from where Pamela lived.

It is too early to prove a link, but the pattern is hard to ignore. A young woman, late at night, near the coast, a stretch of road where a stranger could stop and offer a lift.

A retired Norfolk detective once told me, "We looked at him, but the trail was ice cold. Everything fits except the evidence."

That is the story of half the names in Tobin's shadow. They fit until you try to prove them.

LINDA MILLAR, BRIGHTON, 1988

Linda Millar's name barely exists in public records. She was 21 when she was reported missing from her flat in the spring of 1988. There was no front-page appeal, no national coverage. Just another young woman who didn't come home.

The timing stood out because it matched the period when Louise Kay vanished. Tobin was in the area then, using another name, moving between Brighton and Crawley.

Little is known about Linda's last days. She was seen near the seafront not long before she disappeared. Her body has never been found.

When I asked a Sussex officer if her case had been reviewed under Operation Anagram, he paused before saying, "Let's just say her name was on the list."

That was all he said. But it told me enough.

LISA HESSION, LEIGH, GREATER MANCHESTER, 1984

Lisa was 14 and was at a friend's house one December evening in 1984.

She left around midnight for the short walk home. The next morning she was found strangled and assaulted, just 200 yards from her front door.

The brutality of the attack, the control, the speed. It all felt familiar. Tobin was known to travel widely through the 1980s, taking work wherever he could. There is no record placing him in Leigh, but there is also no record of where he was not. Police told me later they had checked him and found nothing solid. But when you know his pattern, it is hard not to wonder. Lisa's death feels like the kind of attack he could have carried out in a moment of opportunity and rage.

SANDRA FRENCH, BRIGHTON, 1986

Sandra French's name barely makes the papers now. Aged 21 she was last seen leaving a club in Brighton in 1986. A few weeks later her body was found in woodland outside the city. Contemporary reports described it as a sexual offence. Then the coverage stopped. No major inquiry, no follow-up trial, just another young woman gone. Tobin was working in the area around then, using another name. He came and went, leaving little trace. When detectives from Operation Anagram later went back through the old Brighton cases, one told me, "We pulled every file we could find from the eighties. French was in there. We can't prove he did it, but we can't prove he didn't." That line has stayed with me.

By the time I'd finished going through the names, the list on my kitchen table made me feel sick.

Every one of them was real. A daughter, a friend, someone who had just vanished. It didn't look like a coincidence. It looked like a trail.

The south coast was his hunting ground long before Scotland knew his name.

I had covered enough cases to recognise the same pattern. The same kind of victims. The same gaps in police files.

When I'd finished with England, I turned the map north. To Scotland.

MARGARET HOGG, GLASGOW, 1979

The first name that came to mind was Margaret Hogg. She was 17 when she disappeared walking home from a disco in Glasgow in 1979.

The papers called her "a happy-go-lucky girl". It was the

kind of line that filled space but said nothing about what really happened. Her body was found a few days later on waste ground near her route home. She had been beaten and strangled. Her clothes were torn, and her injuries suggested a sudden, chaotic struggle. No one was ever charged.

Tobin was in Glasgow around that time, drifting between jobs. The place matched. The year matched. The only sticking point was the attack was different to his known methods. It was messy and furious, not controlled like his later crimes.

Even so, I couldn't shake it. I wrote her name on the list and next to it, one word. Maybe.

SHEILA ANDERSON, EDINBURGH, 1983

Then there was Sheila Anderson. Her case had already followed me for a few years. Back in 2001, I'd tried to resurrect her story for the *Edinburgh Evening News*.

Sheila was 27, a sex worker from Edinburgh, who was murdered in April 1983 near Leith Docks.

Her body was found beside Salamander Street, battered and left to be discovered by a taxi driver at dawn. I knew the site well; even in daylight it felt desolate.

The police believed a vehicle was involved, that she'd been run down deliberately.

It was an ugly, targeted attack.

When Tobin's name surfaced, I went back to her file.

He'd spent time in Edinburgh, sometimes working construction, sometimes just passing through. The timelines brushed against each other but never locked. The method was wrong too – he killed by control, by concealment. Sheila's death was public, violent, almost retaliatory. For years there was wild speculation her murder had been committed by a police officer, a judge, a sheriff.

Former Deputy Chief Constable of Lothian and Borders Police, Tom Wood, who had been a young constable around the time of the original investigation, still carries the case.

He once told me, "It's one of those that gets under your skin. You don't stop looking." He's right. But he also warned about the damage of wild speculation.

"Every time someone says it was a cop, or a judge, or Peter Tobin, they reopen wounds for those connected to the case," he said.

And he's right about that too. Rumours might placate the public, but they don't comfort the dead.

The deeper I dug, the more I realised that Scotland had its own archive of shadows – cases that pre-dated Tobin but were always hauled out whenever another killer made the news.

Three murders in particular shaped the country's fear in the late seventies.

HILDA MCAULEY, ANNA KENNY AND AGNES COONEY – THE 1977 TRIO.

They were killed within months of each other. All young women, all out for the night, all found strangled or beaten in and around Glasgow.

Hilda McAuley was 36 and was last seen leaving a pub in Rutherglen in early 1977. The next morning a railway worker found her body near an embankment. She had been sexually assaulted and strangled according to court and police records. Her clothes were torn, her shoes missing. The attack was violent and personal.

Anna Kenny was 20. She left the Hurdy Gurdy club in Glasgow that August and never made it home. For years she was treated as a missing person until her remains were found buried in a shallow grave near Arrochymore Point. The burial told detectives something about her killer. He had taken time to hide her, but not enough to care.

Agnes Cooney was 23. She left a friend's house in Coatbridge in December that same year. Her body was found days later in woodland outside the town. She too had been sexually assaulted and strangled. The similarities were impossible to ignore.

The tabloids called them the dance-hall murders and the name stuck because the victims had all been out socialising before they vanished. It gave the cases a cruel kind of glamour, masking the reality of what had been done to them.

At the time, Strathclyde Police could not link the three murders by evidence, but detectives working the files felt they were connected. Years later, when forensic reviews began, attention turned to another man, Angus Sinclair.

Sinclair was a serial killer from Glasgow who, along with his

UNFOLDING THE ANAGRAM

brother-in-law Gordon Hamilton, murdered two teenage girls, Christine Eadie and Helen Scott, in what became known as the World's End murders. The crimes took place in Edinburgh in October 1977, the same year the trio were killed in and around Glasgow. The women were of similar age, the sexual violence was comparable, and the timing was almost identical.

Cold-case detectives believed the pattern fitted, but no DNA ever linked Sinclair to the Glasgow murders. The burial of Anna Kenny suggested planning, but the rest of the attacks were messy and fast. Without evidence, the files stayed open and unproven.

Still, when Tobin was arrested decades later, those names came back. It was as if Scotland had been waiting for one monster to explain every fear that had lingered since the 70s.

I remember hearing callers on radio phone-ins insisting it had to be him. It did not. The patterns were wrong. The women were older, the attacks uncontrolled, the aftermath rushed and messy.

Tobin's killings were different. They showed patience, preparation, planning. The dance-hall murders felt like something else entirely.

In 2006, though, everything unsolved was dragged back into his orbit. Every old file, every unanswered case.

I spoke to a retired Lothian and Borders officer who had helped with cold case reviews after Tobin's arrest.

He told me, "We ran his name through everything, Jane. Every unsolved case we had since the 60s. He pops up in plenty of wrong places, but that's what drifters do. They cast long shadows."

Then he added, "It's not always about finding more victims. Sometimes it's about letting the wrong ones go."

That stayed with me. We are so desperate to make sense of monsters that we start folding other people's stories into theirs.

JACQUELINE GALLACHER, 1996

Jacqueline Gallacher's name appeared later, when the searches began to spread beyond the 70s and 80s.

She was 26, last seen in Glasgow city centre on 23 June 1996.

Weeks later her body was found in a lay-by off the A814 near Bowling. She had been sexually assaulted and murdered.

There was an arrest and a trial, but the verdict was not proven. No one has ever been convicted.

Her case was one of many pulled back out of storage when Operation Anagram started. It made sense on paper. A young woman, alone at night, a violent attack, a body left by a roadside. But there was nothing to tie it to Tobin.

He was known to move through the central belt around that time, working short jobs and changing names, yet there was no link in the evidence.

Still, her name stayed on the list. It showed how wide the net had been cast.

When a serial killer is caught, every old case with even a hint of similarity is dragged into the light again. The truth is most of them do not belong there.

When I finished the Scottish list, my notes were a mess of names and dates.

UNFOLDING THE ANAGRAM

Margaret Hogg, Sheila Anderson, Hilda McAuley, Anna Kenny, Agnes Cooney.

Each one was a woman with a story that never found an ending. Some might have crossed paths with Tobin, most of them probably didn't. But going back through those files reminded me of something important. Scotland's history of violence does not begin or end with one man.

CHAPTER NINETEEN

SORTING FACT FROM FOLKLORE

WHEN OPERATION ANAGRAM finally went public, the phone never stopped. Families called, reporters called, retired officers called. Everyone had a theory. Everyone had a name.

For a while, it felt as though every unsolved murder in Britain had been laid at Tobin's feet. Some of it came from genuine hope, families desperate for closure after decades of silence.

Others wanted notoriety, or to be close to a story that had taken hold of the country. A single name like his is a magnet; it pulls everything loose into its orbit.

The detectives running Anagram looked exhausted every time I saw them. They had hundreds of case files, each one a maybe. Every town he'd ever lived in, every alias he'd used, every hire car, every temporary job.

Each lead meant a new family, a new heartbreak.

They were trying to prove a negative – that he hadn't killed someone – and that's almost impossible.

One senior officer told me, "We can't chase ghosts forever. We could spend the rest of our careers looking for things he might have done, and miss the ones we can actually prove."

Another admitted that Tobin himself took a certain pleasure in the attention. He'd smirk when detectives mentioned new names. He liked being the bogeyman. I saw the same thing happen in the press.

Editors love patterns; they make sense of chaos. Once Tobin became our shorthand for evil, every cold case started to look like his work. The phone calls would start the same way:

"Jane, we've got another one — fits Tobin to a T."

I'd ask for dates, locations, the method, and nine times out of ten, the pieces didn't fit.

But by then, the headline had already written itself. Even now, years later, it still happens.

Social media posts, amateur sleuths, podcasts linking many missing women in Britain to Peter Tobin. I've seen reports say he might have killed up to 50 women.

It's well-meaning, sometimes even helpful, but it also distorts.

If we make one man responsible for every act of violence, we ignore the rest — the unnamed killers, the failures of policing, the fragility of women's safety.

I'm not defending Tobin. He was a sadistic, manipulative killer who destroyed lives and families. But turning him into a myth does something dangerous. It turns him into a story rather than a man who made choices, hurt people, and walked among us.

He didn't invent that danger. He just embodied it.

During one conversation, a retired detective from Sussex told me, "He's not the key to everything. But he might be the key to understanding how everything was missed."

That struck me. Tobin's life showed how a man could move across decades and jurisdictions without leaving a trace that anyone joined up. Different forces, different databases, different priorities.

When Anagram finally pieced his life together, it was almost too late. It wasn't new evidence that changed things, just the way the files were finally read side by side.

By the autumn of 2007, even as the police kept working, the case had also consumed everything for me. I had spent more than a year chasing him, writing thousands of words, driving from Bathgate to Brighton and back again. Some stories drain you. Others define you. This one did both.

That October I left the *Sunday Mail* for *The Scottish Sun*. It should have been a clean break, but his name followed me. It came through tips, quiet calls and the voices of contacts who still couldn't let it go. Operation Anagram was still running then, widening its reach with every new address and every lead that surfaced. The hunt had become bigger than anyone could contain.

For those of us who had been there since the beginning, the questions never stopped. How many homes had he lived in? How many names had he used? How many women had trusted him for even a moment too long?

Det Supt Swindle once said Tobin managed to hide in plain sight because nobody thought to look in the shadows. Because that is what Anagram became – a search through those shadows, a way of giving three young women back their names and pulling a killer into the light.

For the police it revealed more than one man's crimes. It showed what happens when information is locked behind borders and pride. Anagram forced officers to share and to trust that another force might hold the missing piece. It proved that progress only comes when people stop protecting their patches and start protecting the public.

For the press it was a reckoning. We were part of the chase, driven by the same hunger to know, but we made mistakes too. We rushed to fill gaps before the evidence arrived, we told stories while families were still living them. Anagram reminded me that behind every headline there were people still waiting for the truth. It changed the way I worked. I listened more. I wrote slower. I began to see that the job was not just about breaking stories but about understanding what breaks when the system fails.

As the years passed, new names surfaced.

Cases from the 1970s and 80s in Portsmouth, Brighton, and Glasgow were all revisited.

No direct proof was ever found, but the pattern remained impossible to ignore.

At its height, Anagram handled over 1,400 separate inquiries. It became a model for how modern policing could approach cold cases – collaborative, data-driven, and national in scope.

For Swindle, it also remained personal.

He often said the Paisley case had been the turning point, the moment he realised the system itself had to change.

In interviews years later he described Tobin as "totally evil, with no respect for human life," and stressed that the operation had always been about the victims, not the man who killed them.

By 2010 most of the main lines of inquiry were exhausted. The operation confirmed Tobin's movements from the early 1960s until his arrest in 2006. It showed he used at least 13 aliases and lived in more than 40 addresses across Britain.

In the end the investigation ran out of road. No new evidence. No new bodies. No confession. The team still believed there were others, but belief wasn't enough and by 2011, with all known avenues explored, Operation Anagram was officially wound down.

The files were boxed, the analysts reassigned, but the story never really ended. Several unsolved murders were left open for review, but no further charges followed.

Anagram did not solve every mystery, but it changed how major crime investigations were run. It showed that separate forces could work as one and that technology could bridge the gaps where human error once lived.

And for those who had worked on it, the case remained a lesson in what happens when a man is allowed to slip between the cracks of the system and how hard it is to drag him back into the light.

Years later one of the officers told me, "We could never say how many. All we could say was that it wasn't three."

What stays with me isn't the ones we know about. It's the ones we don't. The women who never made it into the headlines.

The families who never got an answer, just the kind of silence and pain that lasts a lifetime.

Detective Superintendent David Swindle said repeatedly that while only three murders could be proven in court, he believed Tobin was responsible for more.

"It didn't go public until after the conviction," Swindle said. "That's when Anagram went overt. Up to that point it was just a hunch, then it became an operation."

He built the team himself. "Because I was a senior officer, I could drive it. That helped overcome the challenges. This had never been done before." The name suited the purpose. "Maybe because I saw it as a puzzle."

When asked what patterns from Angelika's case suggested Tobin might have killed before, he didn't hesitate. "As TAs, – trained assistants on the inquiry – I said, the same indicators that made me look in the first place."

Tobin gave him nothing.

"He never cooperated, and he never claimed to have murdered 48 women. That story came from someone else, and I know exactly who."

The operation grew fast. "We did UK-wide briefings to all heads of CID and linked HOLMES incident rooms. The scale was enormous."

Media involvement was mixed.

"BBC Crimewatch was the turning point for constructive media support," he said.

And when I asked if we'd ever really know how many women Tobin killed, he didn't pause.

"No. Without doubt he's killed other women. He targeted the vulnerable, women in hostels and religious establishments, people no one reported missing. Who's going to report them?"

For Swindle, the end of Anagram marked the close of his police career. He retired that year, later calling it both the hardest and most important work he had ever done.

He continued to speak publicly about Tobin, giving talks to police and victim-support groups across the country. His message never changed.

"Remember the victims," he said. "Angelika, Vicky, Dinah, and whoever else is still out there."

When I think of Operation Anagram now, I see the tired detectives, the maps on the walls, the late-night calls that began with silence before someone said, "We've found something." I remember what it took to get there. Years of missed chances, one man hiding in plain sight, and the determination of a few people who refused to look away.

That was the hunt. And that was its legacy.

***

After years of work, the picture was as complete as it would ever be. Hundreds of files, dozens of names, thousands of man-hours – all leading back to the same handful of truths. Three confirmed murders. Dozens of possibles. The proven victims were known.

Angelika Kluk, Vicky Hamilton, Dinah McNicol.

Their families had faced the courts, heard the verdicts, and watched the man who killed their daughters vanish behind bars.

But the question that had haunted me since the night of his arrest — how many more? — still hung in the air. After years on the crime beat, I'd learned to separate fact from theory, instinct from fantasy.

Tobin lived a transient life — he changed addresses, names, cars, even accents. He blended in. That gave him opportunity, but not omnipresence.

He couldn't have been everywhere, and he wasn't the answer to every unsolved case. When I laid out all the names I'd traced, the pattern looked clearer.

Highly Probable:

Louise Kay. Eighteen years old, Eastbourne 1988. She fits his geography, his method, his pattern of concealment. Even detectives closest to the case admit privately she could be the one they never found. If I had to name a fourth victim, it would be her.

Possible:

Jessie Earl, Pamela Exall, Linda Millar. All within his reach, all matching some aspect of his behaviour. The sexual control, the isolation, the need to dominate and disappear his victims.

If he killed Jessie, it was early enough to explain the evolution of his methods.

If he killed Pamela, it was the first sign of what was coming.

Linda's case sits in that same year as Vicky and Dinah: it's clear he was at his most dangerous then. His control was slipping, but his violence was escalating.

Unlikely but Worth Reviewing:

Lisa Hession and Sandra French. Their cases echo his violence but not his geography. Maybe coincidence, maybe contagion – the way fear spreads once a name like his is in the air.

Almost Certainly Not:

The Scottish files that were reopened in hope more than evidence – Sheila Anderson, Hilda McAuley, Anna Kenny, Agnes Cooney.

Their stories are Scotland's other heartbreaks, unsolved but separate.

Tobin's shadow brushed against them only because the public needed a name to fill the void.

Those women deserve justice of their own, not the wrong man's. It should also be noted that DNA has been found in the Sheila Anderson case and it does not match Tobin.

A detective once said to me, "We think he killed between three and nine. But we'll never get him to tell us which."

Tobin knew the power of mystery. He liked being the name mentioned in connection to every missing girl. He liked the power it carried and admitting to more would have robbed him of that.

Sometimes I think of the Anagram detectives packing up their boxes and closing the case files one by one. Somewhere in that paperwork there are names no one will ever read again. Victims who slipped through the cracks of time and record-keeping, buried not just by their killer but by bureaucracy and neglect. We will never know them.

SORTING FACT FROM FOLKLORE

That's the hardest part – not the murders we can prove, but the ones we'll never even name.

In early 2019, I broke the story that Peter Tobin was dying. It was front page news, of course.

He'd been in and out of hospital for months. The guards at Saughton said he barely left his cell except for hospital runs and while he'd faked illness before, this time even they believed it was real. Cancer doesn't play games.

The families of his victims hoped the end might bring truth. Dan McNicol, Dinah's brother, told me he wanted Tobin to live long enough to suffer and to finally confess what else he'd done.

"He'll go to his grave remembered as a predator," Dan said. "He's got the chance to tell what he's done."

But Tobin never did.

I heard he was keeping a diary – and had fantasies of getting a publisher. I've never heard anything about those diaries since but I believe the police did check his belongings after he died.

Tobin kept the same line he'd always used – that he didn't give a damn about the families. When a prison psychiatrist asked if he'd killed others, he smiled and said, "Prove it."

He had years to tell the truth. He never did.

By 2022, he was a skeleton of himself. The cancer had spread, the pain constant and he died that October in Edinburgh Royal Infirmary, aged 76. The cause of death was bronchopneumonia, vascular disease and prostate cancer. He took every secret with him.

No one came for his body and his next of kin declined in writing to make arrangements. The council paid for a basic cremation at Mortonhall Crematorium in Edinburgh, and his ashes were scattered at sea. This is what happened to Angus Sinclair and Robert Black too.

His books and papers were boxed up in a prison store room, waiting for a family that never came. A year later, they were still there. I have no idea where they are now.

I would imagine if there was anything worth pursuing, the police would have made it public by now.

It was a quiet, shabby and deserving end to a man who'd spent his life destroying everything he touched. No confession. No closure. Just a file marked "deceased" and a list of names that will never be crossed off.

With his death, Operation Anagram also finally closed. What it left behind was one of the most complete offender histories ever compiled in the United Kingdom.

Its lessons outlived him. Major investigations now routinely cross-check national databases. The systems and working methods developed under Anagram became part of modern policing.

For the officers who served on it, the lesson was simple: never assume that one conviction ends the story. For the families of the missing, it remains a promise that someone, somewhere, will keep looking.

Tobin never confessed. He never explained. The answers went with him.

When I finally closed my own file marked Unsolved, it felt like betrayal.

But journalism has limits, just like policing. You can only go

SORTING FACT FROM FOLKLORE

so far before all you have left is conjecture and ghosts. I still have my files. I don't look at them often but I would never throw them out. That's all these stories ever become in the end. Memory. Evidence. A reminder not to forget. Tobin might have taken the answers with him, but the questions still matter.

And what remained were the names of the girls who should have lived.

Angelika Kluk. Vicky Hamilton. Dinah McNicol.

Every time his face returned to the news, the same question followed. Had he killed more?

And another name always rose to the surface.

Bible John.

CHAPTER TWENTY

THE GHOST OF BIBLE JOHN

WHEN TOBIN'S STORY began to lose its grip, another shadow stepped back into view. Not a man, but a name that had hung over Glasgow for half a century.

I last saw George Puttock on 27 October 2022, at his home in Wokingham, Berkshire.

It was an ordinary cold day as myself and our mutual friend, Nick, took the train there from London. George was clearly unwell but pleased to see us and we spent some time with him and his wife, Mavis, who was as kind and gracious as ever.

George was the widower of Helen Puttock, the 29-year-old mother of two who became the third and final known victim of the man Scotland still calls Bible John. Her murder in 1969 was the killing that cemented the case in Scottish criminal folklore and tied the Puttock family to 50 years of unanswered questions.

George said he'd wanted to thank me for keeping Helen's name in the public eye. He never wanted her to be forgotten. I knew it would be the last time I saw him and sadly, George died three weeks later, on 20 November, aged 81.

Losing George hit harder than I expected. We had spoken for more than 20 years, usually when I was working on a Bible John piece or a cold case that brushed against Helen's. In the last two years of his life, we'd spoken at least once a week. George was always gracious with his time and was never annoyed when I asked the same questions over and over hoping for different answers.

George had grown frail, his hands trembling slightly but he was still as sharp as a tack. He still had a quiet dignity about him, the same calm he'd carried through 50 years that came from having survived the worst moment of his life and all the suspicion that followed.

We talked about nothing at first. The weather, Glasgow, how everything changes and nothing changes, how little, really, had changed at all. The conversation always circled back to Helen.

"She's never far away," he said softly. "Not for a day."

Bible John was a killer who slipped into folklore the moment the case went cold.

Every few years, someone would claim to know who he was and every few years, the headlines would flare and die.

George had lived through all of them.

By the end, I think it had exhausted something in him. Late in life he convinced himself Helen was killed by the Yorkshire Ripper. It was not madness, it was grief trying to land somewhere. He spent half a century listening to strangers tell him who murdered his wife. When one theory collapsed, he clung to the next.

"I think it was that Ripper fella," he told me. "He was up there. The police never checked it right."

There was no point arguing. He knew the truth. Peter Sutcliffe – who murdered 13 women and attempted to kill seven others across northern England between 1975 and 1980 – had no link to Scotland. But grief has its own logic, and after decades of nothing, people reach for anything that looks like certainty.

George lived most of his life under suspicion, and even in death, he couldn't escape it. I wrote then what I still believe now: the dead can't defend themselves, so it's the job of those who knew them to do it for them.

Helen's name anchored our chat that afternoon. Even in his last weeks, the need to know hadn't left him, if anything it probably felt more urgent. I was sorry I couldn't give him any answers.

To understand what that meant for George, and for the families who lived with the same pain, you have to go back to where it all began – Glasgow, 1968, and the murders that gave birth to the name Bible John.

PATRICIA DOCKER

In February 1968 Glasgow was still cold enough to burn your lungs. Frost clung to the stone closes in Battlefield. In the morning, the buses hissed along the wet roads, and people hurried to work, their heads down in an effort to protect themselves from the biting cold.

Patricia Docker was 25, a nurse and a mother. She lived with her parents in Langside Place after separating from her husband. It wasn't the life she'd planned, but she was trying to build something stable for herself and her little boy. She worked hard, kept herself neat and tidy, and tried not to care what the neighbours said about a woman on her own with a child.

On the night of Thursday, 22 February, she told her parents she was going dancing at the Majestic Ballroom on Hope Street.

Instead, she went to the Barrowland Ballroom. It was the over 25s night, an older crowd, more respectable, or so people said. The band played familiar songs and for a few hours, she could feel young again.

No one remembered much about who she danced with that night. The police would later trace dozens of people who might have seen her, but nobody could give a clear account. Someone thought they'd heard a woman shouting "let me go" in the dark. Another said they saw a light-coloured car parked nearby. It made no difference to the investigation – they were dead ends.

Patricia left the Barrowland just before midnight. How she got home, no one could ever say for sure. Some thought she walked, others believed she took a lift from someone she knew.

The next morning, her body was found in the alley behind 27 Carmichael Place, only a few streets from her home.

She was naked, her clothes were gone, her shoes left beside her. She had been beaten around the head and strangled with something strong, maybe a belt. The brutality of it stunned even the seasoned officers who first arrived.

Rain had turned the ground slick, washing away much of what might have been evidence. The small back lane, hemmed in by garages, became the centre of a murder hunt that would haunt the city for years. Her handbag and jewellery were missing.

The river Cart moves slowly through the south side of Glasgow. It runs behind tenements and old mills, bordered by stone walls thick with moss. In winter it turns the colour of iron. The water looks still until you watch long enough to see it shift, dark and cold. The river was lined with washing poles and broken fences. Oil from the garages nearby left a film that shimmered when the light hit it. It wasn't a place people lingered. When the police divers first went in, they expected to find nothing.

The current was slow but strong enough to pull at their legs. They worked as quickly as they could, hands sweeping the riverbed. Bottles, branches, old ropes, wood and bits of scrap.

Then one of them surfaced holding a handbag. It was small and dark, the clasp bent, mud packed into the seams.

It was Patricia Docker's. A lipstick and a pair of underwear, believed to be hers, was also pulled from the water.

Police found her smashed watch not far from the spot where she died. Her father identified her body the next day. Reporters waited outside the police station, but he said nothing.

The postmortem confirmed she had been strangled but not sexually assaulted and she had likely died a few hours before she was found. The violence was targeted, personal, but also coldly efficient.

At first, police thought she might have been killed elsewhere and left there later. The incline of the lane meant a car could have rolled down in silence, lights off. It was the kind of detail the detectives held onto when everything else made no sense. Theories multiplied. An ex-husband. A stranger from the dance hall. Someone local. The case never found a single solid lead.

Within weeks, the investigation cooled. Patricia became the first woman in a story no one realised was forming.

JEMIMA MACDONALD

By August 1969, the shipyards were closing, the money had dried up, and people filled the long nights with drink, music, and the promise of company. The Barrowland Ballroom was still at the heart of the weekend world. On Saturday nights it pulled people in from every direction.

Jemima MacDonald lived in Bridgeton, a few miles east. She was 31, a mother of three, and worked when she could. Her sister Margaret often looked after the children so Jemima could have a night out. She was warm, friendly, and easy to like. People said she loved dancing and never missed a chance to dress up.

On the night of Saturday 16 August, she told her sister she was heading to the Barrowland. She wore a patterned dress and high heels. The ballroom was crowded, the band loud enough to drown any chance at conversation but Jemima was seen chatting and laughing with a tall man, well dressed, slim build, in his late 20s or early 30s.

Witnesses said he was polite, well spoken, not rough like most of the men who went there. They danced together for most of the night. Near half past twelve, the two were seen leaving through the main doors, walking towards Main Street. The rain had stopped. That was the last time anyone saw Jemima alive. That night, she didn't come home and Margaret thought she'd stayed with a friend, but by Sunday afternoon the worry had set in. Rumours spread quickly through Bridgeton that children playing in an old building on MacKeith Street reported a terrible smell. On Monday, Margaret couldn't stand the waiting any longer. She went to the derelict tenement herself, climbed the stairs, and opened a door into the darkness. Her sister was lying face down on the floor. She had been beaten badly, her face swollen and bloodied. Her stockings and shoes were beside her. She had been strangled, most likely with her own stockings. Margaret ran out into the street screaming for help. The police came fast, sealed off the building and worked by torchlight. Detectives took photographs. Jemima had been dead for more than a day and the postmortem confirmed she was beaten and strangled.

Like Patricia Docker, she was menstruating at the time of her death.

Her handbag was missing. Neighbours said they had heard screams in the early hours, but no one could give a clear time. Others said they saw her with a fair-haired man near the building. None of the details were enough to build a picture that held.

Jemima's family buried her privately. Her children were too young to understand what had happened. The police called it a savage and senseless killing. The papers called it the Barrowland murder. For months detectives knocked on doors and took statements, but the leads went nowhere.

The case joined Patricia Docker's on a growing pile of unsolved murders. Two women dead. Both last seen at the Barrowland. Both killed with a level of control and violence that seemed deliberate.

No one connected the cases publicly. Not yet.

Then came Halloween 1969.

HELEN PUTTOCK

On Friday, 31 October 1969, rain fell steadily over Glasgow. The glow of the Barrowland Ballroom lit up the mist above Gallowgate, drawing people from every part of the city. Inside, the band was loud, the air thick with smoke and perfume. Helen Puttock was 29, a mother of two boys, living in a ground-floor flat on Earl Street, Partick. Her husband George was home on Army leave.

George wanted Helen to stay in that night but she was used to him being away and she wanted a night out. An argument broke out but Helen was adamant she wasn't staying in. She had been looking forward to going out with her sister, Jean Langford, all week. Jean picked her up and George gave the women money for a taxi home. The dancehall was their escape, a place to dance, socialise and feel visible again – their escape from the boredom of being housewives and mothers.

The band played pop songs, the lights turning the faces on the floor gold and pink. Sometime during that night the sisters met two men, both introduced themselves as John. One said he was a slater from Castlemilk, easy to talk to, a drinker. The other stood out.

He was neater, older, with dark hair and pale eyes. He wore a brown Reid & Taylor suit and a striped tie. He didn't drink, only lemonade, and spoke with a soft Glaswegian accent.

Jean noticed how different he was from the rest. He talked about faith, paraphrasing lines from the Bible as if they were everyday conversation. He spoke of right and wrong, of sin, of how people had lost their fear of God. His voice stayed calm and careful, each word measured.

The four of them kept together most of the evening and when the dancing finished they all made to leave.

Jeannie stopped to buy cigarettes for the next day, but the vending machine jammed and kept her money. Helen's companion took charge. He called the manager over and demanded a refund. Jeannie remembered how calm he was. He didn't shout or swear. His tone was controlled, clipped, almost superior. She said it reminded her of a teacher scolding a pupil. "He gave the manager a proper dressing down," she recalled later. "I thought he'd get a hiding for the way he spoke, but to my surprise the manager backed off."

From the way he handled the situation, she thought he was a man used to giving orders and being obeyed. The manager accepted the machine was faulty but explained that the tills were closed and she would need to come back the next day for her money. At that, John's manner hardened. As they walked downstairs, he told the two women, "My father says these places are dens of iniquity."

Outside, Jeannie's partner caught up with them. When she looked at Helen, her sister was deep in conversation with John.

Helen looked amused, shaking her head and smirking, as if she didn't believe something he'd told her. Then John pulled something from his inside pocket and showed it to her, like he was proving a point. Jeannie thought it looked like a card of some kind. The effect on Helen was instant. Her expression changed from disbelief to trust. Whatever she saw on that card convinced her he was genuine. When Jeannie leaned forward to get a look, John pulled it away and said, "You know what happens to nosy folk." Jeannie later said she believed it was some kind of identification. Helen wouldn't have trusted a stranger unless she thought he was official in some way.

The four of them left the Barrowland and walked along Gallowgate toward Glasgow Cross. At London Road, Jeannie's partner said goodnight and headed for a bus to Castlemilk. Jeannie later said she thought he was married and had given her a false name. He was never traced.

Helen, Jeannie and John carried on together and flagged down a taxi for Scotstoun. The journey started quietly. John sat beside Helen, cold and withdrawn. Jeannie felt he saw her as an obstacle between him and her sister and she tried to break the tension by making small talk, but he gave little away. He said his family had a caravan in Irvine and that he played golf. When she asked if he liked dancing, his mood turned again. He said he didn't approve of married women going to dance halls and spoke harshly about adulterous women. He mentioned having a sister, then changed the subject to life in a foster home. When Jeannie asked how he spent New Year, he said he didn't drink, that he prayed instead.

Moments later, he contradicted himself, saying he was agnostic. Then he began quoting from the Bible. As the taxi passed high flats at Kingsway, he said something about his father or another relative having worked there. Police later noted that a foster home had once stood in that area, and some believed it might explain his familiarity with it. When the cab reached Earl Street, it would have made sense for Helen to get out first.

Jeannie lived further along at Kelso Street. But John told the driver to take Jeannie home first. At the roundabout, Jeannie said goodnight to her sister.

"I'll maybe see you next week," she began, but before she could finish, John slammed the taxi door.

The driver later told police that he dropped the couple at 95 Earl Street a few minutes later. The woman got out, and the man, who he assumed was her partner, paid the fare. The driver thought the man looked annoyed because the woman had walked off ahead of him. He drove off, unaware he was the last person apart from the killer to see her alive.

Around 2am, a Number 6 night bus was travelling along Dumbarton Road toward the city centre. Near Gardner Street, it stopped for a man who looked dishevelled. Another witness had seen the same man walking quickly up the street. On the bus, the driver, conductor and a passenger noticed mud on his jacket and a scratch below his eye. He looked nervous and tried to hide his appearance. To those who saw him, it was clear he'd been in a fight. At Derby Street he got off the bus and disappeared into the dark.

At 7.30am, a resident of 95 Earl Street, Archibald MacIntyre, took his dog out for a walk. In the back court, the dog began sniffing what looked like a bundle of rags. MacIntyre said later, "When I went over, I got a terrible shock. It was a woman's body. She was wearing her coat, but it had been pulled roughly up over her head."

One of her own stockings was tied around her neck. He ran to a nearby phone box and called the police. Officers found injuries to her face and head. There was dried blood around her mouth and nose, and heavy bruising that made her almost unrecognisable. Her dress and coat were torn. A broken gold chain lay near her body and her handbag was missing. In the mud, detectives found a cheap cufflink, likely torn from the attacker's clothing during the struggle. There were bite marks on her wrist. Residents gathered in the courtyard as police tried to preserve the scene. Many stepped too close, disturbing potential evidence. It was the third time in 18 months that detectives faced a murdered woman and almost no leads. A mobile incident unit was parked outside the house and officers began door-to-door enquiries. One neighbour said they'd heard a woman cry out during the night but assumed it was someone drunk coming home from the dance halls.

Later that morning George went to the caravan and told officers his wife hadn't come home from a night out with her sister. He described her clothes and was taken aside by an officer, who said quietly, "I'm sorry, son, your wife's been murdered."

He later told reporters he felt numb, unable to take it in. The policeman walked him back to the house, but he tried to look past them into the alleyway where she lay. They wouldn't let him. As with the first two victims, she had been menstruating. A sanitary towel was found under her arm. The pattern was undeniable now.

CHAPTER TWENTY-ONE

THE HUNT

JEANNIE LANGFORD WAS told soon after her sister's body was found. She was in shock and it took time before detectives could take a full statement. They knew she was their key witness. She had spoken to the man who had almost certainly killed her sister. She told them the man had something pinned to his lapel but she could not describe it clearly, she only remembered that he kept touching it. Sometimes he covered it with his hand, other times he brushed his fingers over it as if it steadied him. She thought it looked like a badge or small pin, the kind of thing that might mean something official, though she could not say for certain.

Jeannie's first description, taken before fatigue and suggestion could interfere, was clear on one point that would later be distorted: she said the man had dark hair, neatly cut, with pale or greyish eyes and a narrow face. Nothing in her initial account suggested the fair or reddish hair that would come to dominate the case.

On 4 November 1969, *The Glasgow Herald* ran the headline: Bible-Quoting Man Sought by Murder Hunt Police.

HUNTING SHADOWS

The police notice gave the public a man aged 25 to 30, 5ft10in to 6ft tall, medium build, with light auburn hair brushed to the right, blue-grey eyes, straight teeth with one tooth overlapping, and smart clothes. This was the point where the description began to shift. The lighter hair came not from Jeannie's original statement but from the sketch that would soon follow.

Jeannie's statement changed the landscape of the investigation. The first two murders had offered no witnesses and no description worth anything. Detectives had been working with theories, not facts, and the hunt went nowhere.

Jeannie was the first person who had sat beside the man and heard him speak.

For the first time, police had a witness.

Her account became the backbone of the investigation. She told them what she remembered from the taxi: his voice, the calm way he spoke, the coldness behind his talk about sin, religion and the state of women. Detectives took detailed notes. When her story reached the press, one detail electrified the public. The man had quoted from the Bible. He had called himself John. The label stuck. Bible John.

Her description shaped everything that followed. She said he was slim, well spoken, in his mid-20s. Dark hair in her early statement, later reconstructed as fair or reddish. A brown or blue suit. A striped tie. The kind of man who blended in. Detective Superintendent Joe Beattie wanted an image the public could hold. He brought in Lennox Paterson, a registrar at the Glasgow School of Art. Paterson was a respected painter but not a police forensic artist. He listened to Jeannie, studied

THE HUNT

her, and produced a drawing based on how he interpreted her words rather than the specific details she had given.

The result looked polished. It also looked wrong.

Paterson's sketch showed a stronger jaw, paler eyes and significantly lighter hair than Jeannie had described. It bore little resemblance to the darker-haired man she remembered in the taxi. But when the picture was produced, it was based almost entirely on Paterson's interpretation. It became the face of the investigation.

From that point onward, detectives were told to look for a tall, polite, fair-haired man who spoke well and might be from outside Glasgow. Dark-haired suspects were sidelined. Leads that clashed with the sketch were dropped quietly. The hunt narrowed around a man who may never have existed.

The artist's impression appeared everywhere. On the front pages of every Scottish paper. In bus stations, in police canteens, in briefing rooms, inside the Barrowland Ballroom. It stared out at a city already on edge.

The press called the hunt the biggest since Bible John's last victim. The public treated the sketch as gospel. Beattie became the face of the investigation. Photographers caught him outside Pitt Street HQ, trilby pulled low, pipe in hand.

They called him Glasgow's last hope. Behind the image, his team were close to burnout. The work was relentless. Every lead required a follow-up. Every rumour required a check. Every scrap of information had to be logged by hand. Detectives worked through the nights and morale thinned out but they kept going.

They interviewed more than 50,000 men. They visited slaters, soldiers, labourers, clerks, bus drivers, priests, students. They checked military postings, employment records, church rosters, school lists and dental files. Taxi drivers were questioned and re-questioned. Witnesses were traced from Ayr to Aberdeen.

Women officers were sent undercover into the Barrowland. They dressed for the floor, nursed lemonades poured into whisky glasses, and scanned every man who approached them. At closing time they walked out alone and were shadowed through the dark streets by colleagues watching for anyone who might follow them. They saw nothing.

The Barrowland changed. The neon lights still flickered over Gallowgate, but the crowds shifted. Women stopped going alone. Taxi drivers became wary. Men watched their friends more closely. Glasgow was used to violence, but this was different. This felt controlled, it felt targeted. It frightened people in a way the usual violence had not.

The other man named John, the slater who had been dancing with Jeannie, was never traced. He never came forward. No one knew whether he had been using a false name or whether he simply disappeared into the churn of everyday life, unaware of the role he had played in the last hours of a murdered woman.

By early 1970 the inquiry was turned back on itself. Statements were re-read. Witnesses were revisited. Files reopened. Detectives circled the same names again and again, hoping fresh eyes would spot something missed. They were still looking for one man, but the face they were following was an artist's invention, not the witness's memory.

THE HUNT

By the mid-70s the investigation was cold. The files were boxed and stored at Pitt Street, where dust settled on the cardboard lids. Years passed. The case that had once filled Scotland's front pages was now silent.

Beattie retired not long after. He kept the cuttings in his drawer. He kept the drawing. He took them out in later years and looked at them, certain the answer was still buried somewhere in the earliest days. In interviews he would puff on his pipe, eyes darkening, and repeat what he had believed from the first week.

Someone knows this man.

He died in 2000, still waiting for a name.

After his death younger detectives reopened the boxes. Three women. The same hall. The same method. The same man who walked out of the night and vanished.

***

By the mid-90s, the Bible John case was three decades old. The faces in the photographs had faded to grey and most of the detectives who had worked it were retired or dead.

When the cold-case team reopened the files, one name stood out. John Irvine McInnes. He had been a young soldier in the Scots Guards in the 1960s, a quiet man with no criminal record and few ties outside his regiment and family.

He was connected by blood to one of the early suspects in the Bible John inquiry and distantly related to a senior police officer. In 1980, aged 41, he took his own life, cutting an artery in his arm. He was buried quietly in Stonehouse, Lanarkshire.

In 1996, long before DNA testing became routine, police were granted permission to exhume his body. The idea came from a mix of rumour, frustration, and the hope that new science might finally close an open wound in Scottish policing. Some believed McInnes could have been the man who left the Barrowland Ballroom with Helen Puttock. Others thought it was a desperate reach by detectives haunted by a case that never found an ending.

When the grave was opened, reporters crowded outside the cemetery gates. Flashbulbs lit the rain. It felt as if the past itself was being dug up. Officers in white suits lifted a bone sample from the coffin and sealed it for testing. For months the country waited and the newspapers ran with it: Bible John at last?

Jean Langford was still alive. She had sat through more than 300 identity parades and never once identified a man. When detectives showed her McInnes's photograph, she shook her head.

"That's not him," she said.

Months later the laboratory results came back but the DNA tests were inconclusive. The technology of the time wasn't advanced enough to confirm or deny a match. The Lord Advocate later announced there was no conclusive evidence linking McInnes to the murders. Official wording was no evidence was capable of implicating McInnes.

The story dimmed but never fully disappeared. A dead suspect who could not speak for himself suited everyone. It gave the illusion of progress without admitting defeat.

A decade later, science had moved on and in 2005, the preserved exhibits from the Puttock file were tested again using more advanced techniques. This time the results were clear, the DNA profile from the crime scene did not match McInnes and he was ruled out completely.

That should have been the end of it but old cases rarely die in Glasgow. The name Bible John still filled front pages whenever a new whisper surfaced. It was part of the city's language – half fact, half superstition.

And then, in 2006, Peter Tobin appeared.

***

By the time Peter Tobin's name appeared in the headlines, Scotland had already spent decades waiting for Bible John to return. When a killer with roots in Glasgow, a church connection, and a violent hatred of women was suddenly unmasked, the theory almost wrote itself. I remember sitting in the newsroom the week Tobin's face appeared on television, the same week the first details about Angelika Kluk's murder began to surface.

"It's him, Bible John," someone said. "It has to be. Look at the eyes."

You couldn't fault the logic. Both men hunted Glasgow, both picked vulnerable women, both lived double lives and cloaked themselves in the illusion of faith. Even the age fits the story if you squinted at the timeline. And the media, desperate for a hook, ran with it.

But stories like that are seductive because they're tidy. Real life rarely is.

When the comparisons began, I went back through my notes. The timelines did not fit. Tobin was 23 in 1969, living between Glasgow and Brighton. He had married Margaret Mountney on 6 August that year, just 10 days before Jemima McDonald was murdered. Margaret later said they were still on honeymoon in Brighton at the time of the killing.

By October, when Helen Puttock died, Tobin and Margaret were living in Brighton. He had a job, a tenancy, and crucially, a paper trail.

DNA sealed it. When a partial male profile was extracted from Helen's tights and compared with Tobin's, it didn't match. Not even close.

That should have ended the speculation, but myths rooted in Scottish folklore don't die quietly. The press and the public had their story and weren't ready to let it go. It was neater to believe one monster had done it all. It gave the illusion of closure.

The problem was, it also gave false hope to families who'd lived with unanswered questions for half a century.

***

When a case grows old and the evidence is thin, the only thing left is to speak to someone who has never stopped thinking. I wanted to test my own instincts against someone who has spent a lifetime studying men like Tobin. Someone who keeps looking for sense where most people have given up. For me, that person is Professor David Wilson. We have disagreed for years about Bible John. David believes Tobin could be him. I do not. Our friendship has survived every discussion and every argument. We often end up circling around the same question. If not Tobin, then who?

David once told me that the point of a theory is not to be right, it is to set out a position that others can challenge. He first wrote about the Tobin and Bible John connection in 2010. He reminded me that it was exactly that, a hypothesis. He wanted readers to test it and try to pull it apart.

He reminded me of something important. "I wrote the book in 2010," he said. "It is making an hypothesis about Bible John and, at the same time, suggesting that anyone else can come forward and disprove that hypothesis. That is how reason and rationality work."

He also said something that has stayed with me. "In many ways trying to uncover Bible John's identity is like howling at the moon," he wrote, "but in trying to do so, I take the original investigation very seriously."

He spoke to detectives who worked the case. "At that time the detectives believed the three murders were linked."

When I asked when he first seriously thought Tobin might be Bible John, he told me it began with the murder of Angelika Kluk. "It was the murder of Kluk that started me on this road," he said. He went to Glasgow with Sky journalist Paul Harrison.

"So much about Angelika's murder just shouted Bible John," he told me.

He listed the things that struck him. "The Church and confessional. The flight afterwards to London. Very geographically mobile. The discovery of Tobin in a hospital. His age and previous offending history."

They then walked the streets where the victims were last seen. They pulled what files were still available. "The research involved walking the streets of the three murders, uncovering relevant files such as autopsies and talking to anyone who was prepared to discuss the case."

When I asked what moved him from maybe to probably, he told me it was an interview with Tobin's wife at the time, Margaret (Mountney) Macintosh. "That swung things," he said.

He described the moment. "On a map of the city, I had marked the sites of the three murders. I put the map down on the floor. She looked at it and said, something to the effect of, 'Why have you marked where my parents lived?' The place she pointed to was the site of the third murder. Tobin had picked her up from that street many times."

Margaret also spoke about Tobin's family and his behaviour as a husband. "Very religious, quiet," she said of his parents.

Of Tobin, she said enough that David simply wrote, "He was toxic."

I asked how much of the theory came from profiling or files. He told me clearly, "Yes, this was mostly about profiling, geo-profiling and looking at Tobin's known offending history." But he did not pretend there was forensic proof. "There was no forensic material that was reliable. It was all frankly degraded and compromised."

Then he added the line he has repeated for years. "That is why the DNA angle seems to me to be a huge error. Clearly there is Tobin's DNA on file, but there is nothing to compare it to from the three BJ murders. Do not believe anyone who tells you that there is."

I asked whether he had seen the DNA work or the 2004 cold case review. His answer was the same. "There is nothing that can be used from the productions of the three victims that would generate a usable DNA profile of anyone."

The biggest weakness in his own theory is the second murder, Jemima MacDonald's. "He was on honeymoon down in England," he said, but Margaret also said Tobin "would disappear for days" including during the honeymoon.

David told me it was possible Tobin travelled back to Glasgow. "That was one of Tobin's signatures," he said. "He was constantly on the move."

When I asked if anything in recent years shifted his view, he said he was interested in the suggestion that the three murders might not all be linked. "That would mean that if we ignore the second murder then Tobin might still have committed the first and third."

The media coverage of the 1960s shaped everything. "It was crucial in creating Bible John," he told me. He did not blame the press. "The Glasgow Police were desperately trying to catch a killer and had to harness media interest." He also reminded me the police had used one of the earliest criminal profiles, produced by Robert Brittain of Carstairs Hospital.

When I asked if the Tobin and Bible John line took on a life of its own, he answered without hesitation. "Yes. Without doubt." But he understood why. "If you were the police and had a series of unsolved murders you had to involve the media. It was like they had a tiger by the tail."

I wanted to know if David, despite his 2010 theory, had

ever found any other suspect credible. He said suspects appear regularly, and vanish just as quickly.

"I keep expecting my hypothesis to be knocked out of the park because a suspect emerges," he said, "but just as they emerge, they fail. Tobin, on the other hand, remains credible."

Finally, I asked if he would stand by the theory today.

"I would be more judicious about linking all three murders," he said.

That is David Wilson. Clear, honest, willing to revise, but never willing to stop asking questions. We will probably argue about this until the end of time, but I will say this: There are very few people in this line of work whose judgement I trust completely. He is one of them.

That does not mean I agree with him. Especially not about Tobin. On that point we are planted on opposite sides and we both know it. David is one of the sharpest minds I know and I respect him enormously and he is one of the few people who can make me question myself – but not on this.

He believes the overlap is too strong to ignore. The violence, the misogyny, the religious fixation – all hallmarks of Tobin's personality.

He once told me, "If it walks like a duck and quacks like a duck…"

I laughed. "Then it still needs a DNA match, David."

He grinned, raised his eyebrows, and said, "You journalists never could resist killing a good story with facts."

"And you criminologists," I said, "never could resist keeping one alive."

THE HUNT

We have even argued about it on David's BBC television show *Crime Files*.

Neither of us will budge from our own theories. It's friendly banter, but it's rooted in something serious. Because to me, the truth matters more than the myth.

Tobin doesn't need Bible John's crimes to make him monstrous. His victims – Angelika Kluk, Vicky Hamilton, Dinah McNicol – are more than enough. And the evidence is unambiguous. Tobin was married and living in England when Helen Puttock died. His DNA doesn't match the partial male profile taken from Helen's clothing. No witnesses placed him in Glasgow at the time. What's left are similarities of style and cruelty, not substance or fact.

When images of a young Peter Tobin first appeared in the media, people began to make comparisons. They said he looked like the man in the artist's sketch of Bible John. The same sharp features, the same style of hair, even the same stillness in the eyes. For many, that was enough. The myth had found a new face.

But in a case rooted in fear and memory, likeness is a fragile thing. The sketch was an interpretation rather than a scientific likeness, produced from a witness's recollection after a traumatic night. In hindsight, investigators questioned how closely it matched the description originally given. Faces change. Memory bends. What people thought they recognised was not truth but familiarity, the comfort of a story that finally seemed to fit.

The evidence never matched. The timelines did not fit. The

DNA ruled him out completely. Tobin might have looked like the Bible John that Lennox and Beattie imagined, but that was where the similarities ended.

George once told me he did not want to sully Jean's memory, but the truth was they had been drinking heavily that night. He said it gently, without blame, only as a reminder that memory is fragile.

Drink, shock and grief distort it further. What seemed clear in the days after Helen's death may have blurred over time, and what police later built their image on might never have been exact.

That should have ended the speculation, but myths never die quietly.

But if not Tobin, then who?

John Irvine McInnes was the man detectives could never quite rule out.

He was the man they could never quite rule out, even though the DNA tests did not match. The sample taken from his exhumation was old, degraded, and handled long before modern contamination controls. While the science said no, many detectives I've spoken to say it's not enough to close the book on him. The 1995 detectives believe McInnes was the man in the taxi with Helen the night she was murdered.

McInnes was the right age, the right build, and the right background. His family links placed him inside the web of the original inquiry, and his death in 1980 marked an ending that felt almost too neat.

I can't prove it, and I won't pretend to.

But if Bible John ever had a name, I think that might have been it.

***

When I first spoke to George Puttock, he wanted nothing to do with me. He'd spent years avoiding reporters and I don't blame him. Every few years, another one turned up at his door, promising sensitivity and leaving him gutted. By the time I came knocking, he'd been burned too many times to count.

We chatted while he weighed me up. I told him I didn't want to write about Helen's murder – not yet, not like that. I wanted to understand what it had done to him.

That earned a flicker of trust.

Over time, he told me what Helen was really like: her laughter, her stubborn streak, her pride in her appearance, the way she danced. He told me about their ordinary life – the quiet evenings, the family gatherings, the plans that stopped at 29.

And he told me what it was like to live for 50 years with people whispering that maybe you were involved.

"They'd look at me in shops," he said once. "I'd see the thought cross their face – him. They think it was me."

Whatever people think they know about Bible John, I know what George was – a man who loved his wife, who grieved her for 50 years, and a man who deserved peace.

Today the police files remain open but inactive. The DNA from Helen's tights – that faint male trace – is too incomplete to identify anyone conclusively. The murders of Patricia Docker, Jemima McDonald, and Helen Puttock are still unsolved.

When David Swindle was asked about it years later, he was clear. "Peter Tobin wasn't Bible John," he said. "The evidence doesn't fit. To link them is to do a disservice to the victims."

He's right. It cheapens truth and blurs justice.

Much of the original physical exhibits and forensic samples from the Bible John murders have since been lost or destroyed. Files were misplaced, exhibits discarded, and key samples degraded with time.

And yet the name endures. Bible John has become part of Scotland's folklore – a story retold in bars, books, and podcasts by people who never met the families, who see the horror as entertainment. The photofit still surfaces online every few months, eyes staring out from the past. The myth keeps breathing because it's easier to live with a monster you can name than one who simply vanished.

Sometimes I wonder if that's the point. Maybe Bible John is less a man than a mirror – reflecting everything Glasgow feared about itself in the late 60s: religion, repression, sex, sin, shame. Maybe he was a man who died unnoticed decades ago, leaving a legend in his place.

Every time I pass the Barrowland, I think about the ghosts still there. Helen. Patricia. Jemima. Jean. Joe Beattie. And George.

The Barrowland still buzzes with activity. After all, life goes on.

Sometimes I think the cruellest thing about Bible John isn't that he got away – it's that he took so many other lives with him, people who never got to stop being part of his story.

I miss speaking to George. I miss his chatter, his dry humour, his refusal to let bitterness take him.

THE HUNT

He once said, "If they ever find him, I don't really want to know. I just want Helen to be remembered kindly."

And that's how I'll remember George Puttock – not as the man shadowed by suspicion, but as a husband who loved and waited, long after the rest of the world moved on.

The case will always divide opinion.

I've learned that it isn't always about winning arguments; it's about remembering who was lost.

Bible John may never have a name.

What stays with me is the people he left behind and what it cost them.

CHAPTER TWENTY-TWO

WIDER SHADOWS – THE WORLD'S END

THE FIRST TIME I ever heard of the World's End murders, I wasn't a reporter, I was a teenager in the passenger seat of my step-father Eddie's car. We were heading down the High Street on Edinburgh's famous Royal Mile – the cobbled spine that runs from the castle to Holyrood Palace, lined with closes, tourist shops and centuries of ghost stories – when he nodded towards a pub on the corner and said, almost casually, "I got called in about that once."

I turned to him, not sure what he meant. He kept his eyes on the road.

"Two girls were murdered," he said. "They were asking a lot of the oil rig boys back then. Blood tests, fingerprints. Anyone who worked away."

He said it as if it were nothing unusual, just one of those things that happened in a city like ours. But the way his voice flattened made me quiet. The name of the place stuck in my head long after we'd driven past: The World's End.

To teenage me, it sounded like a bad place, not somewhere

you'd stop for a pint. I've always had an imagination, but it just looked like an ordinary pub to me. There was no internet back then, so I couldn't exactly look it up. Eddie, despite his comments, seemed reluctant to tell me the story. It was only a few days later, after I'd asked repeatedly, that he finally said their names and how they'd gone to the pub and ended up murdered. That was all I knew.

Years later, when I joined the *Evening News*, those words came back to me. I was a young reporter covering break-ins, court hearings, general local news but I was itching to get into crime.

By 2001 the *Evening News* was based in a glass and steel building at the foot of Holyrood Road, a few minutes' walk from the Parliament that was still taking shape. We shared the place with *The Scotsman* and *Scotland on Sunday*, all owned by the Barclay brothers back then. It looked modern and expensive, the kind of newsroom that made you stand a bit straighter when you walked in, but underneath it still ran on the same old pressure.

The *Evening News* was a three-edition paper. Morning, lunchtime and late. That meant the day never really stopped. Copy deadlines came like waves. You'd file a story, take a breath, then the next edition would need a fresh page lead or an extra quote. Circulation was still strong, close to 100,000, and the paper mattered. If something happened in the city, it went through that newsroom before it reached anyone else.

It was there that the World's End murders stopped being a half-remembered story from my teenage years and became part of my working life. The names Christine Eadie and Helen

Scott weren't just case notes any more. They were shorthand for everything unsolved in the city. You couldn't grow up in Edinburgh and not know those names, but now they were part of the files I was writing about, part of the daily conversation in the newsroom.

Every crime reporter has stories that seem to age with them, cases that never quite leave. The World's End was one of mine. It had shaped the way the city thought about danger. Two friends walking home after a night out, vanishing between one doorway and the next. The story was told and retold so often that people stopped believing it would ever be solved.

I would revisit it whenever the opportunity arose, especially when I was promoted from a general news reporter to the Crime Reporter. That meant I could get my teeth into all the unsolved cases – and this is where my fascination began. The first unsolved cases I worked on for a special pull-out edition were Vicky Hamilton, The World's End, Robert Higgins, Neil McCann and Sheila Anderson. I could not believe how many unsolved cases were still outstanding in such a small area. You think you know your city until you start counting the dead.

By 2003 the *Evening News* was the paper where my fascination with unsolved murders turned into something more serious.

It was a city paper that mattered, and if you wanted to prove yourself as a crime reporter, this was the place.

The World's End story was never far from the surface. In June that year my byline ran over the headline "New DNA hope in World's End hunt." Detectives were preparing to use a new technique that could trace a killer through his relatives. The same process had already solved a triple murder in Wales. It sounded like science fiction then, but the technology was real, and for the first time in years the case felt alive again.

By September it was front-page news. "World's End killings: DNA breakthrough." Forensic teams had found a partial match to the killer's DNA and were preparing to test more than 200 men. For weeks the story dominated every edition and when the Crimewatch reconstruction aired, the phones in our newsroom lit up with new leads. The city was talking again.

I wrote follow-ups for months. One ran under "Machine to speed up DNA tests set for city." Lothian and Borders Police were spending more than £100,000 on new forensic equipment to double the rate of testing. Tom Nelson from the labs told me the new analyser could run 90 samples in a single cycle and pull DNA from traces as small as saliva. It doesn't sound remarkable now, but back then it meant the difference between waiting a week and waiting two days. For detectives chasing a ghost from 1977, that kind of speed was revolutionary.

Then came May 2004. My front page that day read "Serial killer link in World's End murders." It was the biggest development in 27 years.

Police believed the same man who killed Helen Scott and Christine Eadie might also be responsible for five other unsolved murders across Scotland. Lothian and Borders, Strathclyde and Tayside forces joined up under a new banner: Operation Trinity. The man leading it was Deputy Chief Constable Tom Wood.

For weeks I filed daily updates. The next morning's edition

carried "Father of World's End victim speaks of hope." I'd spoken again with Helen's father, Morain who told me he'd learned to stay calm after so many false starts, but this time felt different. He believed the police wouldn't have gone public unless they were sure. "What sort of person can go about with this on their minds for 27 years?" he asked me. It was one of those quotes that stops you cold.

By Monday the phones at Livingston Police Station were ringing off the hook. "Calls flood in over World's End deaths" was the headline that day. People who had stayed silent for decades were suddenly phoning in with memories, suspicions, and fragments of information. The public had woken up. Tom Wood said it was proof the cases never left the country's conscience. Around 100 officers were now working full time on the inquiry, combing through old statements, checking every scrap of paper that might hold a clue.

On Tuesday I wrote a longer feature – "Hunt goes on for killers in unsolved murders" which tied everything together. Tom told me there was no such thing as an unsolved murder, only cases waiting for their next opportunity. It was a line that summed him up. Calm, methodical, no theatre. He'd once worked the Sheila Anderson case in Edinburgh and knew what it meant to carry a file that never closed.

That piece took readers beyond the World's End story to the bigger picture – Scotland's other forgotten victims. Anna Kenny, Matilda McAuley, Agnes Cooney, Carol Lannen, Elizabeth McCabe.

Then local cases that still filled police filing cabinets: the

WIDER SHADOWS – THE WORLD'S END

gangland killing of Neil McCann, the stabbing of Robert Higgins, the canal murder of Ann Ballantine, the disappearance of Vicky Hamilton. Writing it, I realised how many open wounds a small country could hold.

For me it was also a lesson in how news can shape history. Those *Evening News* headlines didn't solve the World's End murders, but they kept them alive long enough for Operation Trinity to take root. Within weeks, Tom Wood's new squad – including senior investigators Ian Thomas, Roddy Ross and Eddie McCusker – were working side by side in Livingston. Readers today might recognise McCusker's name from the 2025 Lockerbie drama – a role that, in police circles, is deemed to be a misportrayal – but back then he was one of the detectives determined to bring closure to families who had waited a lifetime.

Looking back, that week in May 2004 feels like the moment Scotland finally faced its unfinished stories. Forensics had caught up with the past, the police had joined forces, and the public started to believe again.

And for me, sitting in that modern newsroom under the shadow of Arthur's Seat, it was the first time I understood what persistence really looked like.

When I finally broke the story that detectives had a suspect, I wasn't thinking about glory. I was thinking about how long those two faces had waited. I'd got wind of it from a trusted contact – the kind of contact you don't question when the information feels solid. We checked it, argued about how far we could go, and decided to run it. The headline hit the front page before anyone could stop it. The headline read: 'Serial Killer Link in World's End Murders'. We knew from my police contacts they suspected a murderer named Angus Sinclair but we stopped short of naming him that day.

Tom Wood, then Deputy Chief Constable, rang to make his feelings clear. He wasn't happy about the leak, but he didn't slam the door on it either. He knew as well as I did that publicity keeps oxygen in a cold case. Later, when the dust settled, he admitted the coverage helped.

That moment taught me something I've never forgotten: policing and journalism may clash, but sometimes the collision pushes the truth forward.

By the time Operation Trinity launched, I'd moved to the *Sunday Mail*. The newsroom there was louder, brasher, more competitive. But the same tip offs about the World's End murders kept resurfacing. Every few months there'd be a rumour – DNA advances, a sample re-tested. When Sinclair stood trial in 2014, I was outside the High Court for the *Daily Record*, notebook in hand. Fourteen years, four newspapers, the same two girls. The case had grown up with me.

Angus Sinclair was not what people expected a monster to look like. Ordinary looking, careful, the kind of man who could vanish into a crowd. He'd been a painter, a decorator, a husband, a predator. He had already killed before the World's End – an eight-year-old girl in the 60s – but he'd walked free on a technicality and built a life that hid the violence underneath. By the time his name was read in court it wasn't a surprise, I had known it for months. Hearing it spoken in that room only confirmed what I already suspected, that I had been circling the same story for most of my career.

Sinclair's trial was less theatre than reckoning. Years of failed attempts, collapsed cases, and appeals had left everyone cautious but Operation Trinity had been meticulous: hundreds of exhibits re-examined, witnesses re-interviewed, fragments of DNA coaxed from old slides and envelopes. It wasn't the work of one man but of a team that refused to quit. Tom Wood never claimed to be the man who "caught" Sinclair; he always said it was about the collective. Watching him handle the attention, I saw the same steadiness I'd seen years earlier when my story leaked. He hadn't raged or threatened, he understood how easily justice could be derailed. Tom had overseen plenty of my exclusives by then and knew exactly how far I could get with the right lead.

When the verdict finally came, there was no celebration. Outside the court, families hugged and wept. Reporters wrote fast. Detectives looked ten years older. Scotland had its conviction, but it also had its mirror held up.

The case had taken 37 years and a revolution in forensic science to reach that point. One prosecution had already failed. In 2007, Sinclair was brought to trial for the World's End murders, but the case collapsed before it could reach a jury verdict. The evidence was not yet strong enough to meet the legal test, and he walked free of those charges. What followed were seven years of waiting, while the science advanced and the law itself changed. Only then could the case return to court, rebuilt around proof that had not existed the first time.

We had finally caught up with a piece of our own history, but at a cost.

Sinclair's crimes belonged to a time before databases and shared intelligence, when forces guarded information like territory. He was never a local monster. He moved easily across Scotland, choosing victims he could reach rather than the places he belonged. The World's End murders exposed that reality. Sinclair crossed boundaries, adapted, and disappeared into the gaps between jurisdictions. The system did not. He was only finally convicted when science, not speed or instinct, closed those gaps for good.

When I thought back to Eddie's words in the car – how the police had called in rig workers from all over – I understood what he'd meant. The investigation had been a trawl through an entire generation of men who moved. The killer hadn't been protected by red tape or missed connections, he'd been protected by time. Back in 1977, the science wasn't ready. Thankfully, a young forensic scientist named Lester Knibb had the foresight to preserve the samples taken from the girls' bodies. Without him, there would have been nothing left to test. Sinclair didn't outsmart anyone, he only survived through luck and timing.

Sinclair wasn't alone in that. There was another name, one that would soon dominate every conversation about serial killers in Britain.

***

Robert Black was the man in the van. He used his delivery routes to hunt children across the UK, a predator disguised as an ordinary tradesman. By the time police stopped him in 1990 – halfway through abducting another girl – they realised they'd been driving past his crimes for years.

He'd used the same motorways Tobin later travelled, the same rest stops, the same anonymity of movement.

Black's victims were younger, his violence rooted in compulsion rather than control, but the pattern was familiar: mobility, opportunity, invisibility.

I covered parts of that story too. The details were almost unbearable. Parents who'd waited decades for news, detectives who still kept photos of missing children in their wallets. Black turned geography itself into an accomplice. He could leave Scotland in the morning, commit a murder in England by afternoon, and be home before anyone knew a child was missing. The case forced British policing to admit what it had long resisted – that killers don't respect borders, and neither should investigations.

One detective who had worked on both the Black inquiry and Operation Anagram told me years later, "The common denominator isn't the men, Jane. It's the space between them."

He meant the administrative blind spots: the unshared evidence, the unlogged aliases, the missed pattern. But I think he also meant something deeper – the moral gaps, the points where society stops paying attention.

Those gaps were where Sinclair thrived in the 70s. Black followed in the 80s. Tobin slipped through them until the day Angelika Kluk died. Each exposed the same weakness in a different decade.

By the mid-2000s the landscape had shifted. DNA profiling was sharper; old barriers between forces were beginning to crumble. Journalists like me had learned to navigate those changes too. We were no longer told to stay in our lane. Some officers even welcomed us, understanding that a story told well could keep pressure on an investigation when bureaucracy couldn't.

Operation Anagram became the proof of that. Many of the detectives who'd once chased Sinclair or Black came out of retirement to map Tobin's past.

They understood that a lifetime's worth of aliases and movement could hide dozens of unsolved crimes. For them, Anagram wasn't just about one man; it was about closing the national chapter on a type of killer that had haunted Scotland for 50 years.

Standing on the pavement outside the High Court after another verdict, I often thought about that first drive past the pub with Eddie. He'd been right in ways neither of us could have known. Men who worked away, who lived half-visible lives, left wounds that took a generation to trace. He died in 2011, long before Tobin's final conviction, but I think he would have understood the strange satisfaction of seeing these old stories finally end. He believed in doing the right thing quietly and he would have liked to know that the country he loved had learned to look harder.

The truth is, Tobin didn't exist in a vacuum. He was the product of the same blind spots that let Sinclair and Black move unchecked. Scotland's serial killer age wasn't about singular evil; it was about repetition. Every generation inherited its own monster and had to relearn how to see him.

The years after Black's arrest brought a reckoning. The old regional forces – Strathclyde, Lothian and Borders, Fife, Tayside – each had their own lists of unsolved murders, their own forgotten names. Some victims had faded to pencil marks on folders. Others were reduced to single items of evidence sealed in brown envelopes. The creation of national databases promised to change that, but it took people, not computers, to make connections.

Operation Anagram, and perhaps even to some extent, Operation Trinity, was built on that principle. It was less a manhunt than a national memory test: every file revisited, every assumption challenged. Detectives went back through decades of missing persons reports, re-reading statements that had gathered dust.

Journalists like me began tracing our own archives, comparing old headlines, re-checking bylines.

The question was never just how many Tobin had killed, but how many we had missed.

It reminded me of the Templeton Woods murders – the bodies of two young women found in the late 70s, both dumped in the same area near Dundee. For years the cases were linked, and every few years someone new claimed to have cracked them. The truth never quite settled. Each theory revealed more about the investigators than about the killer. That was how it was in Scotland for a long time: we told ourselves stories to fill the space where answers should have been.

Even Bible John – long before Sinclair or Tobin – taught us how myths grow when certainty fades. Every generation had a case like that, a shadow that stretched too wide to contain. By the time Tobin's name became public, those ghosts were already waiting for him. People wanted him to be Bible John, to tie up the loose ends of a half-century of fear. But the facts didn't fit. Tobin didn't need to be anyone else's monster; he was enough of his own.

There was something about the geography of Scotland that made these stories linger. The cities were close, the roads familiar. You could drive from Edinburgh to Glasgow in under an hour, pass through half a dozen jurisdictions, and still feel as if you hadn't left home. The same streets where I'd reported on Sinclair's conviction were the ones where I'd stood years earlier outside St Patrick's Church after Angelika Kluk's body was found. The distances between cases were smaller than they looked on a map.

When you spend long enough covering murder, you start to recognise patterns of habit as much as patterns of crime. The way detectives talk in shorthand. The way neighbours describe a suspect as quiet, polite, "always said hello". The way a country searches for meaning after each new headline. Every case becomes a reflection of the last.

What struck me most about the men who defined Scotland's serial age was how ordinary they seemed. Sinclair, Black, Tobin – all working men, all with families, all moving through public life unnoticed. None of them clever in the cinematic sense, just methodical and patient, they survived by blending in. Their ordinariness was their disguise and that was what made them terrifying: they didn't live in dark alleys, they lived next door.

The systems that failed to catch them early weren't evil or lazy. They were human too – overworked, underfunded, territorial. Each force wanted its own success, each region guarded its evidence. Before computers, that meant handwritten notes and filing cabinets, faxes sent and never answered. When Tobin finally came into focus, it wasn't through luck but through the slow unravelling of those habits. Operation Anagram forced the country to look at itself and ask how many lives might have been saved if cooperation had come sooner.

I remember a conversation with a retired officer who worked on more than one of those cases. He told me he'd spent half his career apologising for mistakes made before he joined. "We were building a jigsaw," he said, "but nobody realised we were all working on the same picture." That stayed with me. The killers weren't connected, but the failures were.

Journalists carried their own share of those failures. In the old days, competition was everything. First byline, first photo, first to doorstep a family and I played my part in that. But somewhere between Sinclair's trial and Tobin's last conviction, the work changed. We learned to hold the space for victims, not just headlines. Stories became more human and the job stopped being about chasing and became about witnessing.

By the time Tobin's health began to fail, Scotland was tired of its monsters. There was no appetite for mythology anymore. The questions had shifted from who killed them to how did we let it happen for so long? The answer was never simple, but it always came back to those same gaps – between forces, between decades, between attention and apathy.

Even as forensic science advanced, human nature didn't. People still disappeared, evidence still got lost, old names still surfaced in new files. The difference was that now, someone was always watching. Every unsolved case carried the echo of those that came before it.

When I look back over my notebooks from those years, I can trace the country's learning curve in headlines. The early stories were full of fear and speculation. Later ones spoke about DNA, databases, and victim advocacy. Somewhere along the line, Scotland stopped whispering about evil and started measuring it. That shift didn't happen in a lab or a courtroom; it happened in conversations – in press rooms, police stations, and family kitchens.

I used to think of these cases as separate. Now I see them as chapters in the same story. The World's End, Templeton Woods, Black, Tobin – they were all part of the same reckoning. Each time the country said "never again" and each time it learned how fragile those words can be.

When Tobin was finally locked away, I didn't feel triumph. Just relief, mixed with a familiar unease. Because you never really know when a story like that is finished. There's always another file, another name, another family still waiting for the truth. The reporters who cover these cases learn to live with that uncertainty and we keep going because someone has to.

Sometimes I think about how different Scotland looks now from the one I grew up in. The old High Street feels cleaner, safer, but the stones still hold memory. I pass the World's End pub sometimes and see tourists taking photos beneath the sign. They don't know what those words once meant here. Maybe that's a kind of progress, or maybe it's forgetting. I'm never sure which.

Eddie would have liked to see it now – the city, the sense of closure, the way his stepdaughter ended up writing about the very case that once brushed against his life.

He never talked much about his own work on the rigs, but he always asked about mine. When he died, I found one of my clippings folded into his wallet. It was actually just something he'd cut out the paper that only showed my byline – Jane Hamilton, Crime Reporter. He'd kept it there, worn at the edges. That's the sort of pride you don't forget.

He taught me that bearing witness matters, even when it hurts. Maybe that's why I stayed with these stories. They were never just about death; they were about persistence – Eddie's, the detectives', the families'. Scotland isn't defined by its killers but by the people who refused to let them fade into the dark.

The shadows never leave, but we learn to walk beside them. That's what we do here: we keep looking.

CHAPTER TWENTY-THREE

COULD THERE BE ANOTHER TOBIN?

WHEN PETER TOBIN was finally caught, people said it was the end of an era. The end of the drifters. Men who could move from town to town with a false name, cash in hand, no record, no phone, no trace. He belonged to a time when you could be anonymous and still have a life. Those days are mostly gone.

Modern policing has made it almost impossible for someone like Tobin to vanish for long. Every car journey, every phone call, every bank transaction leaves a trail. You can't walk through a city centre without being filmed a dozen times. Even the smallest murder investigation now pulls in CCTV, phone data, social media, DNA, and bank records within hours. The world has closed in on people like him.

When Tobin was active, DNA was still in its infancy. In the late 80s and early 90s, samples had to be large and well preserved to yield results. Many weren't. Forensic scientists worked with blood typing, fibres, fingerprints, and witness recall. It was good work, but limited by the tools of the time.

COULD THERE BE ANOTHER TOBIN?

Today, a single skin cell can identify a suspect. Familial DNA can locate a killer through a relative who has never broken the law. In England and Wales, the national DNA database holds profiles from around seven million people. Scotland has its own independent database, smaller but equally efficient, and the two systems cooperate closely through the UK Forensic Science Regulator.

Most murders in Scotland are now solved within weeks and the detection rate has hovered around 98% for years. The remaining 2% are almost always the hardest to prove – missing-body cases, organised crime hits, or historic murders where evidence has degraded.

Statistically, Scotland has one of the best murder-clearance rates in the world. The old spectre of an unidentified serial killer operating for decades has faded because the gaps that once hid them have been filled by data.

That doesn't mean serial killers have vanished, they've just changed shape.

In recent years, the headlines have shown how quickly patterns can still slip through the cracks. Stephen Port killed four men in London between 2014 and 2015 before police realised the deaths were connected. David Fuller, an NHS electrician from Kent, murdered two women in 1987 and wasn't identified until 2020, when a cold-case DNA review matched him to the scene. Both men were caught not through witnesses or confession, but through science finally doing what humans had missed.

Cases like those remind us that killers don't stop adapting. Port used dating apps. Fuller hid behind respectability. They moved through a society that prides itself on safety, and still managed to kill. The tools have changed, but the instincts are the same.

The difference is that now, technology eventually catches up. There's always a trace – a digital footprint, a biological fragment, a recorded journey. What takes months or years to detect is no longer whether a crime happened, but how soon it can be proved.

The United Kingdom's approach to homicide investigation is now built on the lessons of men like Tobin. HOLMES II, the national police database, connects forces across the country. It flags patterns, names, addresses, vehicles, and timelines. When a murder is logged, analysts check it against others for similarities. A man using a false identity can no longer count on distance to save him.

If Tobin had killed in 2025, he would have been flagged within days. CCTV from church grounds, mobile-phone pings, digital payments, even an old employer's HR system would have exposed him.

In Scotland, the shift has been even sharper and the creation of Police Scotland in 2013 unified resources that were once scattered across eight regional forces, each with its own rhythm, priorities and character.

It had been that way since the early 19th century, when Glasgow became the first city in the country to form a professional police force in 1800. Edinburgh followed five years later. Over time, small burgh and county forces spread across the map. They were built for their surroundings. City police handled crowds, crime and chaos. Rural constables dealt with poaching, theft and family disputes.

By the middle of the 20th century, Scotland had more than 30 separate police forces. It was messy but local, and people knew their own officers by name. The system was eventually streamlined, and by the 1970s it became eight regional constabularies: Lothian and Borders, Strathclyde, Grampian, Tayside, Fife, Central, Dumfries and Galloway, and Northern.

Each had its own chief, its own culture, and a degree of independence. But they all answered to the same laws, and they all learned to work with each other when it mattered. Lothian and Borders Police, formed in 1975, covered Edinburgh and the surrounding counties, stretching from the capital's streets to the quiet border towns. Its headquarters at Fettes Avenue became a symbol of Scottish policing.

The force built a reputation for professionalism and pragmatism. Edinburgh's politics and festivals brought high-profile events. The Borders demanded community policing. Balancing both gave the force an edge that was human as well as strategic.

During the 1980s and 1990s, Lothian and Borders handled some of Scotland's biggest cases – the World's End murders, the disappearance of Vicky Hamilton, and countless other investigations that shaped the country's criminal history. It was a force that understood partnership. Detectives, press officers, and reporters could argue all day, but there was trust underneath it.

People like Noel Miller and Ruth MacLeod – press officers for the force in the 2000s – were more than gatekeepers.

They were the bridge between the police and the press. They answered calls, shared what they could, and said nothing when they had to. That wasn't stonewalling. It was professionalism. They understood that the press wasn't the enemy. Our job was to keep the story alive, to make sure the public stayed aware, to hold attention when memory began to fade.

That partnership mattered. It kept pressure on investigations and helped families believe their cases weren't forgotten. It was never cosy, but it worked because everyone knew their role. Journalists and detectives were part of the same chain, trying in different ways to drag truth into daylight.

By 2013, the old structure was gone and instead merged into one national body: Police Scotland. It was meant to bring efficiency, consistency and savings. And in some ways, it did. Technology improved, information flowed faster, and resources could be moved across the country in hours. But something else was lost in the process. Local knowledge, the kind that came from knowing every back lane and family name in a patch, began to fade. The bond between local reporters and senior detectives thinned too.

The phone calls became emails, the conversations shorter, the walls higher. The job was still about solving crimes, but the humanity that once sat behind it felt further away.

Tobin wasn't clever, but he was careful. He hid in plain sight because no one looked close enough for long enough. That's what makes stories like his so dangerous. They show how easy it is for evil to pass as ordinary. It took years, mistakes, and a lot of people refusing to give up before the truth caught up with him. That's why these stories still matter. They show us what happens when no one joins the dots.

But for all its early teething problems and long-term problems of local policing, the merger did make murder investigations faster and more consistent. Specialist Major Investigation Teams can now deploy anywhere in the country within hours. Forensics are centralised at the Scottish Crime Campus at Gartcosh, a facility that didn't exist when Tobin was killing. Every murder scene, from Glasgow to Inverness, can be analysed with the same equipment and oversight.

The country's size and interconnectedness mean information travels quickly. A missing-person report in Fife will be visible to detectives in Ayrshire the same day. That wasn't the case in the 1980s or 1990s, when separate systems meant a name in one force area could sit unnoticed in another for months.

If Scotland's record on homicide detection is impressive, it's because lessons were learned the hard way. Tobin, Robert Black, Angus Sinclair, and others exposed the weaknesses in communication that once let predators roam. Those gaps are now sealed and the next generation of detectives is trained to look for patterns across regions, not within them.

Yet for all the advances, policing still depends on people. Machines don't interview witnesses or comfort families, algorithms can't read guilt in a pause or instinct in a statement and mistakes still happen because human beings still make them.

The murder of Sarah Everard in England, by a serving police officer, was a reminder that technology can't protect against corruption or arrogance. The murders of Bibaa Henry and Nicole Smallman showed what happens when bias infects procedure – officers taking selfies beside the bodies, evidence mishandled, families ignored. Those aren't failures of science. They're failures of culture.

And journalism is far from immune from it...

Once, the gatekeepers of crime stories were editors and courts, now, the gatekeepers are algorithms.

I saw a young woman on TikTok explaining the Tobin case with confidence that came from nowhere. Half a million views in a day. That is more than most newspapers get in a week. She was sitting on her bed, fairy lights behind her, talking to the camera as if she had solved Scotland's biggest murder inquiry with a few Google searches. Hundreds of comments called her 'brave' for exposing a serial killer. I did not feel angry. I just felt old.

The change is not only about speed, it is about authorship. When I started, a story had to be earned. You worked your patch, built trust, checked the court lists, and waited for the right call. Every line went through lawyers and editors. If you made a mistake, you owned it, but you also corrected it. Victims were named with care – which meant checking and triple checking it was right but also sometimes you had to swallow the editor's decision to wait until the victim had been named officially before you could make it public.

Now a story can travel from Google to video or Facebook in under a minute, wrapped in confidence but light on fact. The digital age did not kill journalism overnight, it just loosened the shoogly bolts that were holding it together.

COULD THERE BE ANOTHER TOBIN?

The demise of newspapers didn't happen overnight either. First the photographers went, then the subs, then the specialists. It used to be all the major courts in the land were covered by agencies and their reporters would know every sheriff, every clerk's name. Some agencies still exist but not a lot – and their staffing levels are sometimes down to one reporter to cover both sheriff and high court cases.

Gone are the veterans who could read a detective's face before a word was said. Gone is experience and empathy and the knack for getting to the bottom of a difficult story or puzzle. What replaced them was not bad people, just a system that prized clicks over craft. Engagement became more important than accuracy. Emotion replaced evidence. That shift did not just affect how stories were told. It changed which stories were told at all.

In the early 2000s, before social media, a crime like Angelika Kluk's murder followed a clear path. Police statement. Verification. Legal checks. Publication. Every fact had a source, every quote had a record. Now a single clip can set a whole narrative running before the truth is confirmed. It is not that people stopped caring about victims, they just stopped waiting for process. They wanted answers fast, they wanted closure, and the internet promised it. But truth takes time, and time is the one thing the online world does not allow.

The Nicola Bulley case showed exactly how far that shift had gone. When she disappeared in January 2023, it became a national story within hours. But it wasn't the police or the press leading it. It was TikTokers, YouTubers and self-proclaimed 'citizen investigators'.

They filmed themselves walking through her village, knocking on doors, combing riverbanks, livestreaming from the exact spot where she was last seen. People picked apart her private life, her partner's expressions, even the way she smiled in photographs. Every day brought a new theory, most of it wrong, all of it invasive. The real reporters tried to cover it properly, but they were drowned out by noise. The police struggled too. Every update they gave fed the speculation, and every silence was treated like a cover-up.

When her body was found, the frenzy stopped for a moment, then it turned on itself.

Blame landed on the police, the press, the family. The same people who demanded updates accused them of saying too much. It was a lesson in how fast compassion curdles online. That case showed what happens when attention replaces accuracy. There were cameras everywhere, but very little truth. The story didn't die when she did, it just moved platforms.

Clips of her final days still circulate online, strangers still argue about what happened.

It proved that information without discipline isn't justice. It's noise.

True crime has become a genre. It has its own market, it creates careers and there is nothing wrong with that. The appetite for reading about crime has always been there. I have written hundreds of features, news stories and books about crime myself. The difference lies in how you handle the story. Journalism is meant to work with the system, not around it. A journalist is bound by law, by fairness, by the duty to

COULD THERE BE ANOTHER TOBIN?

confirm. A content creator is not. That is not arrogance. It is responsibility.

When I write about Tobin, I am accountable to the families, the police, the courts, and the reader. If I get it wrong, someone pays for it. Usually the people who have already lost the most. That is what separates storytelling from exploitation.

When a book I wrote called *My Mother's Murder* came out, Gina McGavin, the victim's daughter, sent me a link to a video using her mother's name for clicks. It was made by someone who had never read the transcripts or spoken to her.

They took fragments of her mother's story and twisted them into a montage – and also littered the video with mistakes. Gina said it felt like her mother's memory had been tainted and tarnished by a stranger who didn't care or respond when Gina complained. That is what happens when truth becomes property. Writing about crime and making a living from it is not exploitation. Taking someone's pain and using it for attention is. That is the difference between journalism and content.

The digital world did not invent the fascination with killers. It just found a faster way to sell it. The old tabloids were guilty of their own excesses. I was part of that world too and we did not always get it right, but we knew what the limits were. We learned from families. We learned from mistakes. The internet does not learn, it just refreshes the page.

Sometimes I think about how the Tobin case would have played out if social media had existed in 2006. The pew, the priest, the missing girl. It would all have been online within hours and almost certainly all wrong. Strangers would have turned it into theories and arguments before the police had even made an arrest. By the time the trial began, half the jury pool would have seen his name online.

The system that once protected the process is now fighting for its life. Contempt of court used to mean something. It still does, legally, but online it has no teeth. A post can reach a million people before a single lawyer reads it. This is not progress, it is chaos.

The truth is still out there, but it is competing with everything else. Facts and feelings share the same feed. People say it is democratic. Maybe it is, but when accountability disappears, accuracy goes with it.

There are still journalists who do the job properly. They turn up. They sit through trials, even the boring bits. They take notes when everyone else has gone home. They get shouted at by lawyers, ignored by police, and still come back the next day. Most of them will never be famous, but without them, the record disappears.

I have watched brilliant reporters walk away. Years of experience lost overnight because there is no money left to keep them. Newsrooms that once held a hundred people now hold 10. Courtrooms that once had a press bench now have an empty space where it used to be. Few write down what happens anymore unless there is a viral headline in it.

That is what scares me the most. Not the trolls. Not the conspiracy theories. The silence. When nobody is there to witness what happens, the facts start to vanish. A court case unreported is a story half-told. A murder unrecorded is a life forgotten.

COULD THERE BE ANOTHER TOBIN?

Real journalism is not about catching killers. It is about preserving truth. It is about fairness and memory. It is about asking the questions nobody else wants to ask. That is the part of the job that still matters.

The public think we make money out of murder. Most of the time we make very little. What we do make is a record. A line in history. That is what endures when the notoriety fades away.

The internet made everyone a storyteller, but it also made everyone forget that stories have consequences. Words can harm. So can silence. The difference lies in intention.

When I sit down to write about Tobin, I do not think about clicks. I think about Angelika, Vicky, and Dinah. About the detectives who spent years chasing shadows. About the families who waited for answers. That is who the work belongs to.

It is not nostalgic to say that the job has changed. It is a fact. The paper stacks are smaller. The deadlines are shorter. The budgets are gone. But the principle is the same.

Be there. Ask questions. Tell it straight.

I meet young reporters now who ask if the job is still worth it. I tell them yes. If you care about truth and people, it is. You might never trend, you might never be thanked, but your work will matter in ways that clicks never can.

Because even in this new world of filters and noise, someone still has to stand in the cold and write down what really happened.

That is journalism. That is what keeps the truth alive.

CHAPTER TWENTY-FOUR

CUTS, CUTS, CUTS

THE CHANGES IN journalism echo in policing and crime investigation too. Budget cuts have stripped local divisions of experience. Senior officers retire early, replaced by younger ranks still learning the craft. The Major Investigation Teams are stretched thin and forensics labs run on deadlines that grow tighter every year.

The risk today isn't that another Tobin is out there killing unnoticed for decades. It's that a future Tobin slips through the cracks for a while because the system is under strain.

Criminologists like Professor David Wilson have argued that the profile of the serial killer itself is changing. The old idea of the drifter or loner is fading. Most modern serial offenders are rooted – they operate within a fixed area, using familiarity instead of anonymity to control victims. They don't need to travel hundreds of miles, they use phones, messaging apps, online marketplaces, dating sites. Their hunting ground is digital.

In that sense, Scotland's next Tobin might not drive a van or bury bodies under a floor. He could live online, exploiting isolation, grooming victims, hiding behind usernames.

The policing challenge now is speed and the internet moves faster than procedure. Warrants take days; predators act in minutes. Detectives can track a suspect's phone, but once a conversation shifts to encrypted apps or the dark web, the trail cools.

The new threats aren't living in halfway houses – they're on the internet.

There are still unsolved murders linked to Tobin's timeline. Louise Kay vanished in 1988 near Eastbourne. Jessie Earl's body was found in 1989 at Beachy Head. Both cases remain officially unresolved. Forensic teams have re-tested evidence several times with newer methods, but degradation, time, and lost samples limit what can be done.

Those failures haunt investigators because they prove that even now, justice depends on preservation and persistence. DNA can work miracles, but it can't resurrect what wasn't collected properly in the first place.

Cold-case units in Scotland continue to review older murders using new techniques. Operation Trinity, the umbrella review of unsolved killings, re-examined dozens of cases. Some, like the 1984 murder of Mary McLaughlin, were finally solved after decades. Others, like the disappearance of Jennifer Kiely or the murder of Karen Roach, remain open but hopeful.

What has changed is expectation. Families now know that science can keep working long after the headlines fade. That belief in time and technology didn't exist 30 years ago. When you ask modern detectives if another Tobin could exist, most say no – not for long, not in the same way.

A man might kill once or twice before being caught, but to sustain a pattern across years, through multiple identities, across borders? Unlikely. The data net is too tight, the systems too joined up. The margin for error has shrunk to almost nothing.

What hasn't changed is motive. Control, humiliation, sexual violence, resentment – those impulses don't vanish with technology. The only difference now is that the warning signs are easier to see, if anyone is looking.

Scotland's murder rate today is among the lowest in Europe, and its clearance rate among the highest. That's not luck. It's structure, training, and a culture of joined-up investigation. The Major Investigation Teams are backed by national intelligence, specialist forensics, and cross-border cooperation with England and Europe. The smallest trace can lead to a conviction.

The real challenge is resource. A brilliant system still fails if there aren't enough people to use it.

The truth is, we probably won't see another Peter Tobin. Not because evil is gone, but because the conditions that sheltered it have changed.

There will still be killers, but they will be caught faster, their worlds smaller. They will leave trails they can't erase.

Tobin was a product of his time – a man who thrived in the gaps between systems. Those gaps have closed. What's left are the lessons. The need for vigilance, the value of communication, the importance of never assuming the worst is over.

Because the moment a society believes it can't happen again, it opens the door for the next man to try. For all the talk about technology and progress, it's the old cases that show what has really changed. You see it best when time runs long and science finally catches up.

Take Elaine Doyle. She was 16 when she was murdered walking home from a disco in Greenock in 1986. She lived with her parents, a quiet girl with a wide smile. Her body was found less than 100 yards from her front door. She'd been sexually assaulted and strangled. It was a case that tore the town apart.

Detectives worked around the clock, they interviewed hundreds of men, door-to-door enquiries filled notebooks. But the killer stayed hidden. There was a trace of DNA, but in 1986 it wasn't enough to identify anyone and the case went cold.

Decades later, a new generation of officers at Strathclyde Police reopened it. The evidence – carefully boxed and stored – was sent for retesting using techniques that didn't exist when Elaine was killed. This time, it spoke. The DNA was matched to John Docherty, a neighbour who'd lived only streets away at the time of the murder. He was a father, a partner, and by all accounts an ordinary man.

In 2014, 28 years after Elaine's death, he was convicted and sentenced to life in prison. It was one of Scotland's longest-running murder investigations, solved because someone believed an old exhibit was still worth testing. That's what science can do when the evidence survives and the will is there.

Elaine's mother, Maureen, said afterwards that she finally felt her daughter could rest. The detectives who had retired came back to sit in the public gallery. It meant something to all of them – proof that persistence and preservation still matter more than luck.

The same truth carried through Emma Caldwell's case.

Emma was 27 when she was murdered in 2005. She had been working in Glasgow's sex trade, often sleeping rough and struggling with addiction. Her body was found in a forest near Biggar. I remember being down at the crime scene on that day for the *Sunday Mail*. Everyone expected it to be solved quickly. At first, detectives arrested four Turkish men and they spent months pursuing that line until the case collapsed for lack of evidence. The real killer was still free.

It took almost 20 years, multiple reviews, and public pressure before the truth emerged. A BBC documentary and reporting by the *Sunday Mail* forced the investigation back open. In 2021, police charged Iain Packer, a former lorry driver who had been known to Emma and was linked to other serious sexual offences.

His trial exposed the mistakes made early on – leads ignored, assumptions made, evidence sidelined. Packer's name was mentioned to detectives within weeks of Emma's disappearance, but never fully followed up. It wasn't new DNA that solved her murder, it was persistence and accountability. The kind of slow, grinding work that doesn't make good television.

In 2023, after 18 years, Packer was convicted. For Emma's family, it was justice long delayed but not denied. For the police, it was a lesson in how easy it is to miss the truth when bias takes over.

Not every story ends that way. Some still sit in the dark.

On a November night in 2004, Alistair Wilson, a 30-year-old bank manager, was shot dead on his doorstep in Nairn while his wife and two young sons were inside the house. The gunman handed Wilson a blue envelope with the word "Paul" on it, then shot him three times. No one knows why.

The gun – a rare Haenel Suhl pistol – was found discarded in a nearby drain, but it yielded little forensic evidence. Over the years, detectives have pursued hundreds of leads, travelling to Canada, the United States, and across Europe. They have cross-referenced DNA, re-examined digital records, and interviewed new witnesses. The case has been reviewed multiple times by Police Scotland's Major Investigation Team but still, no clear suspect has ever been named.

The Wilson case is a reminder that even with every modern advantage, some murders resist answers. Science is powerful, but it can't conjure motive or memory.

Together, these three stories show the range of what Scotland's justice system has become. Elaine Doyle's killer was caught because DNA endured. Emma Caldwell's because people refused to give up. Alistair Wilson's remains unsolved because human nature is harder to decode than any genome.

Forensic breakthroughs have transformed Scottish policing, but the real progress lies in how the country handles its unsolved cases. Cold-case reviews are now routine. Evidence storage is standardised, samples preserved indefinitely. Families are kept updated, not forgotten. Detectives who once retired with regrets now watch new teams take their place.

The difference between now and Tobin's day isn't just technology. It's an expectation. People believe their cases can still be solved. That belief keeps the pressure on. It stops files gathering dust.

Scotland's record supports that optimism. The creation of the Scottish Crime Campus at Gartcosh, the integration of forensic databases, and the sharing of intelligence across borders have made murder the least escapable crime in the country.

That doesn't mean killers have vanished, it means they run out of road faster.

Tobin thrived in the space between investigations, in the years when no one joined the dots.

Those gaps have closed. What's left are single tragedies, not patterns. The country still has blood on its hands, but not the kind that stains for decades.

Every generation believes it's safer than the last. The truth is, safety is just awareness. Scotland is good at catching killers because it never stops looking. The next Tobin is unlikely. The next victim is not.

For all the progress, there are still limits. Technology can find blood in a car boot or match a single hair to a suspect, but it can't see what makes someone dangerous. That part still belongs to instinct and experience.

Machines can't read lies, they can't hear what's missing from a witness statement or sense when a family has stopped believing the police. The science works, but it needs people who know how to use it.

Scotland's detection rates are among the best in the world, but success hides strain. Fewer detectives are doing more work. Major Investigation Teams cover wider ground with smaller budgets. Forensic services face backlogs. Good officers leave early because they're burned out. Progress has a cost.

Cold cases rely on preservation, but preservation costs money. Exhibits need storage, refrigeration, cataloguing, retesting.

That means funding, and funding means politics. If budgets tighten, evidence suffers, and history repeats itself. It only takes one lost box to undo decades of work.

The danger now isn't another Tobin hiding in plain sight. It's complacency, it's assuming technology will do the job for us. When police forces or governments start believing the system is foolproof, mistakes creep back in.

Tobin slipped through the cracks because people stopped looking. He changed names, changed towns, left behind unpaid bills and bruised women, and nobody joined the dots. It wasn't a lack of science, it was a lack of attention. That's still the weak point in every investigation.

If there's a legacy to men like him, it's the reminder that evil doesn't need darkness anymore. It only needs distraction.

The science now is extraordinary. A cigarette end can speak after 40 years. A fingernail can put a man in prison for life. But the real power is in curiosity in someone deciding not to let a file close. Every solved cold case begins with a question that someone refused to stop asking.

That's what Scotland has learned. The country still gets it wrong sometimes, but it doesn't stop asking. Cases like Elaine Doyle's and Emma Caldwell's prove that persistence is stronger than time. Alistair Wilson's case shows that patience still has work to do.

The next Tobin won't get far. The next set of failures might look different, but they'll come from the same place –

overconfidence, exhaustion, and the assumption that we've seen it all before.

We haven't.

The science will keep improving, but it will never replace the human need to notice. That's where real justice begins – in the small act of paying attention.

CHAPTER TWENTY-FIVE

THE WEIGHT OF WITNESS

THERE IS A cost to seeing too much. Every reporter, detective and court clerk knows it, even if we do not say it out loud. You start out believing you can keep the work separate from your life. You cannot.

The faces, the photographs, the statements build up until they form a kind of background noise. It is not trauma in the way people imagine, it is accumulation, the slow weight of other people's worst days. Reporters and police live in the same rhythm: grief, deadline, repeat. You learn to talk about murder over takeaway coffee and make jokes that would sound cruel anywhere else. It is not disrespect, it is survival. Every profession that handles death finds its own language, ours just happens to be written down.

To witness is to absorb. Even when you try to stay detached, something sticks. It is in the way you scan a crowd or how you brace when the phone rings late at night. It is either bad news from home or another body. You remember faces you only saw once. That is the weight of witness. It is not danger that damages you. It is what you cannot turn off.

Behind every headline are hundreds of stories. I have broken more than I can count: murders that changed laws, cold cases reopened, families who finally knew what had happened to the people they loved. But no one carries those stories alone. They pass through the same chain of people who see more than they should. Other journalists, editors, photographers, police, forensic staff, court officers. All witnesses in their own way.

I was never the only journalist looking at Tobin. That wouldn't be true to say. Journalists across different newsrooms had been circling the same questions, at different times, often without knowing what others were seeing. Some worked in print, some in television, some moved jobs and took the story with them.

There was no coordinated effort and no shared theory, just a gradual recognition that this was not a murderer who had arrived fully formed in a Glasgow church. People like Dave Cowan, then at *STV*, Norman Sylvester now at *The Daily Record*, and freelancer Marcello Mega. There are many more across print, television, tabloids, broadcasters – all working in parallel, testing what we were being told against what didn't quite fit.

When Operation Anagram was launched, it moved quickly and decisively, on its own terms. But the attention on Tobin didn't stop there. From that point on, journalists continued to revisit his past, his movements and the unanswered questions that remained. Not as a single investigation, and not with a shared theory, but as an ongoing act of scrutiny that has stretched from those first weeks in 2006 through the years that followed and into the present day.

The difference is what journalists do with what they see.

For reporters, the work ends in print. For the police, it ends in a file. For families, it never ends. The public sees a verdict, a photograph, a line of copy and thinks that is the story. It is not. The real story is the people who keep showing up, year after year, doing work most of the world would rather not think about.

The longer you stay in this job, the more you see how much everyone is carrying. It takes a bit off everyone. The cops go grey. The snappers stop talking. The reporters pretend they are fine. The harm does not come from just the blood or the horror, it comes from the responsibility of telling it right, giving it shape and trying not to make it worse.

You cannot do this work for decades without it changing you. But it is a fair trade. Someone has to look, someone has to write it down.

When I started out, no one talked about what a story did to them. You got it, filed it and moved on. We were not short on compassion, we were trained not to show it. I thought detachment was professionalism. It was not cruelty, just ignorance. I believed distance was strength, that it kept me sharp. It did not, it only made me blind.

Something shifted over time. Maybe it was the first time I saw a mother look at a photograph of her murdered child and still thank me for coming to see her. Maybe it was a courtroom scream that stayed in my head for weeks. I cannot name the moment, only the realisation that followed. Every name in my notebook was a life, not a headline.

I began to see how our words could either deepen pain or bring a kind of peace.

The arrogance of being first fell away, what mattered was being right and being fair. I stopped chasing only the shock and started paying attention to the people at the centre. I listened longer. I wanted to tell the truth without adding to the damage.

That was when the job stopped being about proving myself and started being about doing it properly. Bearing witness is not standing at the edge of tragedy. It is standing in the silence afterwards and writing what you saw with care.

Empathy only matters if it shapes how you work. The real discipline is not the deadline, it is restraint. Knowing what not to print, what not to show, and when to stop asking questions. Editors want colour. Readers want detail. But silence has its own truth. Sometimes the most honest thing you can do is leave space.

Bearing witness is not about emotion, it is about precision. You observe, you listen and you write it as it was, no more and no less. When a family trusts you with their story, you owe them accuracy, not sympathy. When police share something off record, you owe them integrity, not favours.

Restraint became a form of respect. You can tell when a reporter has learned it. The copy is clean, the tone steady, the compassion silent but present. You know they have seen enough to understand that tragedy does not need adjectives.

Some call that detachment. It is not, it is control, the ability to stay balanced in other people's chaos. Without it, you burn out or turn cold. That balance is what separates good reporting from voyeurism. It is also what keeps faith with the families and the public. They do not need drama. They need truth that stands up when everything else has fallen apart.

THE WEIGHT OF WITNESS

We tell ourselves it is just a job, but that is only half true. The other half is what you take home without realising it.

I have watched police age 10 years over one case. I have seen photographers who cannot talk about certain assignments because the images never left them. Court clerks who flinch at names they have heard too often. Reporters who joke too loudly because it is easier than saying they are tired of death.

The public never sees that part. There is no medal for it, no therapy on expenses. You build your own coping mechanisms and hope they hold. Some leave. Some harden. Some learn how to keep caring without breaking. The best of them still feel something every time and that is the real measure of endurance in this line of work. Not how long you last, but how much humanity you manage to keep.

In the end, the weight does not crush you. It settles. It changes how you see the world. You stop asking why bad things happen and start asking how, and what can be done after. That is what bearing witness really means. It is not about death or danger or headlines. It is about recording what happened so it cannot be denied later.

Everyone in this world carries a piece of it home. Police, reporters, lawyers, even court staff. Nobody calls it trauma, but that is what it is. A thousand small shocks that never get talked about. You learn to live with it the way a soldier learns to live with an old wound. It is not weakness. It is the cost.

The pay is poor, the hours are long and the praise, when it comes, feels misplaced. But the work matters. It builds the record, a stubborn archive of truth that says someone saw this and cared enough to write it down.

Every story adds to that record. Every victim named, every injustice exposed, every mistake corrected. It is not about heroics. It is about accountability. Without it, the bad guy wins.

The weight of witness never leaves you, but it teaches you something. Looking away is a privilege and not everyone gets to take it. The rest of us keep looking, that is the job.

Bearing witness is only half the task, the other half is remembering why it matters. After the files close and the headlines fade, what remains are the stories, the proof of what happened and what was learned. That is why we keep going, why we keep writing, why we refuse to forget.

Because if the weight of witness shapes us, its meaning is what keeps us standing.

The longer you do this job, the more you realise it's not just about news. It's also about memory.

Stories fade faster than the people who lived them. Headlines come and go, but grief stays. I've seen that in every front room, every court corridor, every mother's face that has stared past me and whispered, "Just tell it right."

That's what I've tried to do. Tell it right.

When I was young on the job, I thought that meant writing it fast and writing it first. I thought the front page was the prize. But years of standing outside crime scenes and trials beat that out of me. You can't sit through murder after murder and think you're just covering the story. You're part of it, whether you like it or not.

I used to believe strength meant keeping emotion out of the copy. Then I met people whose lives had been torn apart and realised strength looks very different. It's a mother standing outside court, shaking but steady. It's a detective who refuses to retire until a name is cleared. It's a family waiting 16 years for a body to come home.

That's why these stories still matter. They show us who we really are when life cracks open.

When Angelika Kluk was murdered, Scotland was stunned for a week. Then the news cycle moved on. When Vicky Hamilton and Dinah McNicol were found buried together, people read the headlines, shook their heads, and turned the page. That's how news works. But the truth of those crimes didn't end when the cameras left.

It went on in the families who still set an extra plate at Christmas, in the detectives who couldn't sleep, in the journalists who couldn't stop replaying the interviews in their heads.

This book is about that truth. About the damage that lingers, the mistakes that haunted us, and the people who refused to let it go.

It's also about what we didn't see. About how a man like Peter Tobin could move through communities for decades, blending into the wallpaper of ordinary life. A neighbour, a handyman, a husband, a father. A killer hiding in plain sight. And the real question isn't how he did it, it's how no one stopped him sooner.

That's why now matters. Because we are still missing people. Because there are still files gathering dust on shelves. Because every time we decide we've had enough of bad news, someone like Tobin wins.

I didn't write *Hunting Shadows* for nostalgia or shocks. I wrote it because we are losing our appetite for truth. We are numbed by headlines and entertainment dressed as journalism. True crime has become something people binge before bed. But these aren't stories you should sleep easily after. They should unsettle you. They should make you look twice at what gets forgotten.

This book is a reminder that behind every case file is a life. Behind every monster are the cracks we ignored. Behind every police failure are lessons that still matter.

The first lesson is that evil doesn't look the way we expect it to. It doesn't always have the face of a stranger. Sometimes it wears a workman's jacket and a smile. Tobin got away with murder because he knew how to play normal. He charmed landlords, fooled priests, made women feel sorry for him. He relied on the fact that most of us don't believe evil can live next door.

The second lesson is that institutions forget faster than families. I saw it too many times. Police retire, files close, and the system moves on. But mothers don't.

That's what Operation Anagram tried to fight. It was built on the belief that it's never too late to ask again. It proved that persistence works. Anagram was never perfect, but it mattered and it proved that journalism could do more than expose, it could push, prod, and remind the system of what it missed.

I've been asked more times than I can count why I still write about killers. Why give them more attention? The answer is simple. Because their victims can't speak, and silence lets monsters thrive. Writing about them isn't glorifying them. It's documenting their damage. It's pulling the truth out into the light so that no one can pretend it didn't happen.

I've sat through trials where the air felt too heavy to breathe. I've watched jurors turn pale as pathologists described what a body endured. I've stood outside courtrooms waiting for verdicts that could never bring peace. It's easy to say you get used to it, but you don't, you learn how to mask it, how to keep your hands steady enough to type.

Behind every good reporter is a pile of sleepless nights and memories they wish they could unsee. Every cop, every lawyer, every paramedic carries their own version of that. We all pretend we're fine. Most of us aren't.

The truth is that crime never ends with a verdict. The families keep living it. The reporters keep writing it. The detectives keep revisiting it. The story keeps echoing. Every year I still get messages about old cases. Someone saw something. Someone's cousin mentioned a name. Sometimes it's nothing, sometimes it's a door cracking open again after decades. That's the thing about truth. It has patience.

Journalism has changed. The job's different now. Smaller newsrooms, tighter budgets, more work for fewer people. But the job is still the same: to witness, to question, to remember. Not every reporter gets to do that now. Some are too busy chasing clicks to chase truth. But if this book proves anything, it's that the old way still matters. Sitting in someone's living room with a notepad and a cup of cold tea, listening. Walking streets until the story starts to make sense. Caring enough to keep going.

Because caring is the difference between reporting and repeating.

Every time I've told this story over the years, people have asked how I can still bear to write about him. The answer is that I don't write for him, I write for the women he silenced, for the families who still look out the window at night and wonder what else he got away with, for the detectives who didn't sleep until they were sure he'd never walk free again.

And I wrote it because the same patterns are still happening. Women are still disappearing, cases are still mishandled, evidence still goes missing, the public still forgets too fast. You only have to look at the latest headlines to see that we haven't learned enough.

Tobin's story is not just history. It's a warning.

When I look at Angelika, Vicky and Dinah, I don't see victims. I see evidence of what happens when society turns away from the uncomfortable. We talk about danger like it lives in alleyways and dark corners, but it's often hiding in plain sight. These women didn't walk into danger carelessly. They were living ordinary lives, they trusted the wrong person for a moment. That's all it takes.

This book is a map of those moments. How chance, timing and arrogance let a killer move unseen. It's also a record of what people did right. Detectives who refused to give up. Journalists who kept asking questions even when editors lost interest. Families who kept pushing until someone listened.

That's why I decided to write this book now. Because we

are living through another age of distraction, where truth competes with noise. People say there's too much darkness in the world already. They want lighter stories. But ignorance isn't peace, it's permission. Turning away doesn't stop violence, it hides it.

If you want to understand who we are as a country, look at how we treat the missing, the murdered and the forgotten. Look at how we protect women who come forward. Look at how we listen to families when the system fails them. That's where our values live. Not in speeches or slogans, but in whether we keep looking when it's easier not to.

There's a line that stayed with me from an interview years ago. A father whose daughter had been murdered said, "You reporters, you get to go home. We don't." He was right. But that's exactly why we have to keep writing. Because we can go home. Because we have the voice, the platform, the reach. If we don't use it, who will?

I don't believe in closure. I don't believe time heals all wounds, but I believe in the truth. I believe that putting facts in the open changes things. I've seen it happen. I've watched cold cases thaw because someone dared to look again. That's what this book is really about. Persistence.

The truth doesn't disappear. It just waits for the right person to notice.

The stories in these pages don't belong to me. They belong to the people who lived them, the ones who died, and the ones who fought to be heard. The story doesn't stop here. Someone else will keep digging.

If you've read this far, maybe that someone is you. Maybe you'll remember a name, or look twice at a news report, or ask one more question. That's how stories like these change things. Not through shock or spectacle, but through attention.

We can't afford to look away. Because the next Angelika, the next Vicky, the next Dinah is already out there. Somewhere, someone knows something and hasn't spoken. Somewhere, another predator is relying on silence.

Memory is fragile. Truth needs a voice. Because we can't leave history to the killers.

Every word I've written comes down to this. We keep telling these stories so that the lost are not forgotten, and so that the living pay attention. We tell them so that the next time someone vanishes, we recognise the signs sooner. We tell them so that justice doesn't depend on luck or headlines.

We tell them because light only matters if we keep shining it into the dark.

That's why these stories still matter. And that's why we can never, ever turn away.

But that's not to say there isn't a price to pay…

EPILOGUE

I'VE COVERED MURDER for more than 25 years. Hundreds of cases, every kind of victim and every kind of killer. I've stood outside crime scenes in the rain waiting for a name that would change everything. I've watched families crumble when the knock finally came. It never gets easier.

When Peter Tobin was arrested, I was there from the start. From the first missing-person appeal to the search at the church, through the trials and the long years after. I spoke to the people who knew him best: the women who lived with him, the detectives who hunted him, the officers who tried to build a picture of a life spent on the run.

That access mattered. It meant I saw how close he came to being missed again and how often the system looked the other way. I kept going because the story would not leave me alone.

David Swindle, who led Operation Anagram, once called me "the journalist who haunted and was really good at her job, to the point of collecting all the clues about Tobin." He understood the obsession that comes from seeing what others overlook.

This book comes from those years of questions. From interviews, case files, and notebooks filled with times, places, and half-answers. From sitting across from people who wanted to forget and couldn't.

It is not about glory or hindsight. It is about record keeping. About putting down what really happened before it gets rewritten again. Tobin was not a mystery or a legend.

He was a man who blended into everyday lives while everyone else looked elsewhere.

I have spent my career in the space between what the public sees and what really happened. That is where this book lives.

And that is where I have always worked.

ACKNOWLEDGEMENTS

BOOKS LIKE THIS don't happen alone and I've been very lucky to have some remarkable people beside me.

To Clare Fitzsimons, my editor and calm voice when the pressure built. Thank you for every chat, every note and every bit of patience. You have been a rock when this writer felt she wasn't capable! I love working with you and your team.

To Claire Brown, publicist extraordinaire! Your energy and support is second to none! Thank you!

To Christine Costello, for turning chaos into something readable! Your talent is remarkable and you definitely make me look like a better writer than I am. Thank you!

Thanks to Alan Simpson who jogged my memory banks and helped fill in the blanks.

To Ruth M, my lovely friend who reads everything and somehow manages to make me feel like I'm not too bad at this writing lark.

TW. It's hard to believe we've been friends for a quarter of a century. From police headaches to proper friendship, what a journey we have had and I wouldn't change a thing. We've seen a lot in our time. Thank you for contributing to this story! Here's to another 25 years!

To my mum who doesn't always understand what I'm doing but has never stopped believing I could do it.

To my darling husband who has kept the world spinning while I disappeared into work. I couldn't do life without you.

To Sharon Bairden who comes to every event and always cheers me on. Thank you!

To my friend and author Douglas Skelton, who is always on the end of the phone (or messenger) whenever I'm having a mini crisis of confidence or unsure of this world of books. Thanks for always being there, Douglas and for your opinions, advice and guidance which I value greatly.

To Emeritus Professor David Wilson, thanks for the years spent gossiping, laughing with me, arguing with me, putting the world to rights and answering every one of my questions, even the stupid ones. We never tiptoe around each other. We give as good as we get, and our friendship has earned its place. Thanks for adding your voice to this story, even though we don't always agree. You're a true friend.

To David Swindle: Thank you for helping to clarify some points and for always being kind to me about Tobin and my work.

This book reflects years of reporting, questioning and revisiting a story that never truly went away. But I wasn't the only journalist doing that work.

From 2006 onwards, others kept returning to Peter Tobin and the unanswered questions around him, often independently, sometimes crossing the same ground.

I want to acknowledge journalists including Dave Cowan, Norman Sylvester, and Marcello Mega, along with many others across print and broadcast who stayed with the story long after

ACKNOWLEDGEMENTS

the headlines moved on. We didn't work as a group and we didn't share conclusions, but the persistence mattered.

I also want to thank my proofreader, Nick Webster, whose forensic attention to detail strengthened this book at every stage. Their challenges, corrections and insistence on accuracy improved the work immeasurably. Any remaining errors are mine alone.

Although I did not approach the families of Dinah, Angelika and Vicky, and others whose stories appear in these pages, that choice was deliberate. It was made out of respect for the private grief that follows public tragedy. I hope this account treats each woman with the dignity she deserves, and acknowledges the long road to justice faced by their families.

And last but not least to my grandchildren who bring the light and laughter and who have waited patiently while I finished this book. Let's make more memories!